STARTING A LEARNING ASSISTANCE CENTER

Conversations with CRLA members who have been there and done that!

Editors:
Frank Christ
Rick Sheets
Karen Smith

Preface by Mike O'Hear

College Reading & Learning Association

Monograph

H&H Publishing Company, Inc.
1231 Kapp Drive
Clearwater, FL 33765

H&H Publishing Company, Inc.

1231 Kapp Drive
Clearwater, FL 33765
(727) 442-7760
(800) 366-4079
FAX (727) 442-2195
www.HHPublishing.com

STARTING A LEARNING ASSISTANCE CENTER
Conversations With CRLA Members Who Have Been There and Done That!

Editors: Frank L. Christ, Rick A. Sheets, Karen G. Smith

Production Editing
Karen Hackworth, Priscilla Trimmier

Production Supervision
Robert D. Hackworth

Business Operations
Mike Ealy, Sally Marston

Copyright © 2000 by H&H Publishing Company, Inc.

ISBN 0-943202-72-8

Library of Congress Catalog Number 99-97216

All rights reserved. No part of this book may be reproduced or transmitted in any form or by any means, electronic or mechanical, including photocopy, recording, or any information storage or retrieval system, without written permission of the publisher.

Printing is the lowest number: 10 9 8 7 6 5 4 3 2 1

PREFACE

By Mike O'Hear, 1998-99 CRLA President

Starting a new Learning Assistance Center is a daunting task. No matter the size of the operation or the level of support, there is so much to do, so many decisions to make. Which programs need development? Which have moderate to poor potential for success on campus? Which steps will likely insure success potential with faculty and students? How will I gather the staff needed? Will these staffers be full-time, part-time, professionals, students?

More basic questions of center mission and goals need be answered as well. Long term problems, including where the center should ultimately be housed, are also important. Help dealing with these problems is essential for those moving into a director's position for the first time. But even if an individual has directed a center before, each school and program contains enough differences that help in dealing with them can make life easier.

When I was named director of the English Language Skills Lab at West Virginia State College in the early 1970's, there was little help available. I had previously served as the head of a small English Department, but that experience carried few clues to help. Luckily, I had acquired a mentor, Lila Bruckner, then head of the University of South Carolina's reading/study skills program. I had studied under her for a year and found her willing to visit and provide advice; even more importantly, she introduced me to the Western College Reading Association (now the College Reading and Learning Association), which has provided a great deal of help and inspiration through the years.

When I moved to my current job as head of Transitional Studies at Indiana-Purdue Fort Wayne, the situation was greatly different from the one I had experienced in West Virginia. Instead of only reading and writing responsibilities, I had acquired some math responsibilities, a tutoring operation, and the need to work very closely with three academic departments in two different schools. There was a lot to learn, and again mentors became important. In both new situations, I would have profited greatly from a book with information on a wide range of areas that could help in forming questions and action plans. Providing such information is the purpose of this book.

Primary editors Frank Christ, Rick Sheets, and Karen Smith, all experienced LAC directors, have identified a number of areas that are primary concerns in LAC management and have invited a wide selection of long-time LAC personnel to respond to these areas of concern. Contributors include: Gwyn Enright of San Diego City College, Elaine Burns of Skyline College, Frank Torres from California Polytechnic University Pomona, Sylvia Mioduski and Reed Mencke from the University of Arizona, David Gerkin of Paradise Valley Community College, Gene Kerstains, a founding member of CRLA, Martha Maxwell of M.M. Associates, Georgine Materniak from the University of Pittsburgh, as well as myself, Frank, Karen, and Rick.

Areas covered include: LAC definition, professional development, LAC justification, identification of significant individuals, meeting expectations, special populations, faculty roles in LACs, useful management tools, technology, program assessment, student assessment, program types, choice of appropriate instructional resources, staffing, organizational structure, design considerations, image development, and national standards. The book ends with a series of thought-provoking scenarios that cover a range of decision areas facing LAC directors.

All chapters are arranged in question/answer format with experts responding to concerns raised by a moderator. The questions hit on areas of concern to people starting or developing LAC programs. The answers are generally in conversational style as respondents give their views on each of these important areas. The book serves as a primer on matters of importance to LAC directors. Those charged with developing and administrating are, as always, well advised to follow up on the information provided here by joining professional organizations and their sponsored special interest groups on LACs. Attending national or regional conferences put on by these organizations remains a major help in establishing networks and passing on ideas to deal with specific situations that arise as part of LAC development.

Enjoy the book! Learn from it! Raise further questions on the book with its editors and contributors! Use it as a stepping stone in developing a successful LAC.

Mike O'Hear

Introduction

This monograph was conceived as a series of conversations between CRLA members who have had extensive experience as directors of Learning Assistance Centers and younger, less experienced CRLA members. The conversationalists do not have all the answers. Answers will reflect an individual's views based on their experiences with learning assistance centers. Some of the answers are shorter than others as you would expect in an informal setting. In addition, conversations are sometimes interrupted with listener questions when clarification is needed.

CRLA authors/conversationalists include among its most experienced contributors, Martha Maxwell, founder of the first annual institute for learning center directors and staff and author of many important books and articles relevant to learning assistance; Frank L. Christ, one of the founders of CRLA when it was known as WCRA, director of the Summer Institutes for Learning Assistance Professionals at CSU Long Beach and founder and co-director of the annual Winter Institutes for Learning Assistance Center Directors and Staff; Gene Kerstiens, another founder of CRLA and the founder and former director of the Learning Assistance Center at El Camino College in southern California; Gwyn Enright, who has the distinction perhaps of being the only professional who has been a director at both a large state university and a urban community college; Karen Smith, probably the only person who has designed, developed, and directed comprehensive learning centers at a state university (New Mexico State University), a private university (Tulane), and a multi-campus research university (Rutgers) with six learning centers; and Rick Sheets, former founder and director of the Learning Assistance Center at Paradise Valley College and co-director of the Winter Institutes. Contributors include five past presidents of CRLA: Frank Christ, 1968-69; Gene Kerstiens, 1971-72; Karen Smith, 1983-84; Gwyn Enright, 1987-88; and Michael O'Hear, 1998-99. Contributors have over 250 years experience as directors of learning support centers in higher education.

Each conversation ends with a brief biographical sketch of its author. Titles of suggested readings for additional information can be found at the end of most conversations with a full bibliography located as an appendix at the end of the conversations.

NOTE: Because web site URL's change frequently, Internet references are not cited in this monograph. However, the major web site for Learning Support Centers in Higher Education can be found on the Internet at this URL:

http://www.pvc.maricopa.edu/winterinstitute

Starting with the publication release date of this monograph, this web site will have a special section devoted to any additions and changes including an email address to send your comments and suggested readings. Look under RESOURCES/Learning Support Center Resources/Books/Learning Support Centers or use the search bar and type in the phrase "Starting a Learning Assistance Center."

Frank L. Christ, Rick A. Sheets, Karen G. Smith

Contents

Preface by Mike O'Hear	iii
Introduction	v
Question #1: What Is a Learning Assistance Center? *A conversation with Gwyn Enright*	1
Question #2: How Can I Develop My Professionalism in Learning Assistance? *A conversation with Karen Smith*	7
Question #3: How Do I Answer Faculty Members or Administrators When They Ask Why We Have a Learning Assistance Center on Our Campus? *A conversation with Elaine Burns*	13
Question #4: Who Are the Significant Individuals, Units, and Departments That May Support a Campus Learning Assistance Center? *A conversation with Frank Torres*	17
Question #5: How Do I Support Different Expectations of Administration, Departments, Faculty, Students, and Special Units? *A conversation with Sylvia Mioduski*	23
Question #6: What Is the Role of the LAC with Special Populations? *A conversation with Sylvia Mioduski*	29
Question #7: What Is the Role of Faculty in the Development and Operation of LAC Programs and Services? *A conversation with Michael F. O'Hear*	35
Question #8: What Management Tools May Be Useful for the Success of LAC Programs and Services? *A conversation with David Gerkin*	41
Question #9: How Can Technology Enhance the Programs and Services of the Learning Assistance Center? *A conversation with Rick Sheets*	47
Question #10: How Do I Assess What Programs and Services Are Needed for Our Students? *A conversation with Gene Kerstiens*	51

QUESTION #11:
WHAT KINDS OF PROGRAMS AND SERVICES DO LAC'S OFFER?   55
A Conversation with Martha Maxwell

QUESTION #12:
HOW DO I CHOOSE AND USE APPROPRIATE INSTRUCTIONAL RESOURCES FOR STUDENTS?   59
A Conversation with Frank Christ

QUESTION #13:
HOW DO I ASSESS THE NEEDS OF INDIVIDUAL STUDENTS?   63
A Conversation with Reed Mencke

QUESTION #14:
HOW ARE LEARNING ASSISTANCE CENTERS STAFFED AND MANAGED?   69
A conversation with Rick Sheets

QUESTION #15:
HOW WILL THE LAC FIT INTO THE INSTITUTION'S ORGANIZATIONAL STRUCTURE?   77
A conversation with Gwyn Enright

QUESTION #16:
WHERE ARE LAC PROGRAMS AND SERVICES LOCATED?   79
A conversation with Gwyn Enright

QUESTION #17:
WHAT ARE SOME SPACE, FURNISHINGS, AND EQUIPMENT CONSIDERATIONS IN THE
DESIGN OF THE LAC?   81
A conversation with Karen Smith

QUESTION #18:
HOW CAN LAC PROGRAMS AND SERVICES BE EVALUATED?   87
A conversation with David Gerkin

QUESTION #19:
HOW DO I DEVELOP A FAVORABLE IMAGE FOR THE LAC AND HOW DO I PUBLICIZE
THE PROGRAMS AND SERVICES OF THE LAC?   93
A conversation with Frank L. Christ

QUESTION #20:
ARE THERE STANDARDS FOR LEARNING ASSISTANCE PROGRAMS AND SERVICES?   99
A conversation with Georgine Materniak

APPENDIX A:
TYPICAL SCENARIOS OF A LEARNING ASSISTANCE CENTER ADMINISTRATOR   103
Scenarios by Karen G. Smith & Rick A. Sheets

APPENDIX B:
BIBLIOGRAPHY AND ADDITIONAL READINGS   109

QUESTION #1:
WHAT IS A LEARNING ASSISTANCE CENTER?

A conversation with Gwyn Enright

When I was Director of the Learning Resource Center at California State University Northridge in the mid-1980's, I was exceptionally proud of what I did and consequently I talked a lot about the learning center, even to those who were not colleagues. "Wha da ya mean, learning center? Isn't the whole school s'pozed to be a learning center!" heckled a scientist-friend. Ironically, I think a learning assistance center can be defined partially by its philosophical *separation* from the institution.

The learning assistance center is the place students can go for help when, for whatever reason, they are not functioning well in the context of the established institution. At the 1994 Annual Winter Institute for Learning Center Professionals in Tucson, Arizona, I said that 25 years of reading, writing and thinking about learning centers led me to conclude that the fundamental feature of the learning center definition was a *sense of place*.

What an intriguing idea! How did this "sense of place" come to be?

When Frank Christ defined Learning Assistance Center in 1971, he began his definition by saying first that the LAC was "a place." When I borrowed his definition to have a yardstick for tracing the origins of the Learning Assistance Center in 1975, I wrote that the LAC was "a place concerned with learning within and without, functioning primarily to enable students to learn more in less time with greater ease and confidence; offering tutorial help, study aids in the content areas and referrals to other helping agencies; serving as a testing ground for innovative machines, materials, and programs and acting as campus ombudsman." I believed territory or real estate central to the learning assistance center concept. I said the place and its ecology distinguishes the learning assistance center from the isolated reading improvement class, the exhortatory study skills seminar, the glad-handing summer orientation, and the one-shot tutorial session.

So, what does this mean to a student?

Because of who the learning assistance center client is—the student uncomfortable in the academy—he or she requires a place to go to for study skills advice, more information, alternative delivery modes, and answers that go beyond "the party line." Because much of this student's experience in school may be in classrooms and offices where he or she does not feel welcome, I thought it was important to provide a refuge. And so in addition to orchestrating all possible resources to help this student succeed, serving as campus ombudsman is part of my LAC definition. Then I saw the learning assistance center as a place where the student could find scholastic and emotional support, a chair or sofa, and sometimes a cup of coffee.

What about now?

I am rethinking the need to have such a concrete definition of a learning assistance center. Frank Christ, in 1988, proposed a bare bones learning assistance center in which a trained professional can meet with a student or teacher and, using a telephone, an information data base, and a dependable referral system, offer help to improve learning. A virtual learning assistance center, existing only in cyberspace, may be possible if all participants—tutors, counselors, instructors and clients—understand and protect the main functions of a learning assistance center. The learning assistance center welcomes all learners, pulls together and organizes necessary resources—either in one spot or through referral and follow-up—and retains enough independence to address student issues fairly.

How can a learning assistance center be effective if it is independent from the institution?

Well, you've raised a non-trivial issue. Most learning assistance center professionals work conscientiously to integrate the center into the campus community—either through services that cut across departments, such as offering testing or make-up testing; programs that improve instruction on campus, such as faculty development workshops or special faculty consulting; or through locations that bring the centers out from the back lot or up from the basement in order to be visible and convenient in the center of campus. I think these efforts are great and improve the learning assistance center. What I mean by "independence" or "separateness" is a philosophical stance in which the learner and his or her concerns come first.

Gwyn, is "learning assistance center" a generic name for these programs, and if so, how do I select a name for my center?

I don't think it matters. The local origin of the learning assistance center, the campus politics and the tastes of the center director dictate the title of the learning assistance center. Two colleagues and I surveyed all institutions of higher education in the United States in 1975, and we found Learning Assistance Centers mainly in student services at four-year institutions and Study Skills Centers or Reading and Learning Skills Centers mainly in academic departments such as English or Psychology at two-year institutions. We found Learning Resource Centers in the library. Since then, learning assistance centers have undergone much cross fertilization, and specific considerations of architecture, finance, program, personality, and politics at the college or university housing the learning assistance center have had more influence over naming the Center than any need for consistency in the professional literature! The learning assistance center I directed at San Diego City College was, and still is, called The Independent Learning Center because it was located in the library and had a resources emphasis. But the most important reason for the ILC title was that the learning assistance center at Mesa College, another college in our community college district, already had established a learning assistance center called The Independent Learning Center. Its director served on the committee establishing the new Center at City College and on the committee hiring me as the new director!

The multiplicity of names and the embedding of learning center functions within different structures can be confusing, especially to someone new to the field of learning assistance management. Look at Burn's diagram summarizing the "pure" components of a learning assistance center in her article in the *Proceedings of the Winter Institute for Learning Center Professionals*. You can also locate another helpful source in the *Proceedings* in Kerstiens', "A Taxonomy of Learning Support Services."

A favorite activity of veteran learning assistance center professionals, after budget, evaluation, staff, and program are under control, is to debate the differences between learning assistance centers, learning resource centers, and developmental education. Incidentally, not everyone agrees: the debate goes on.

Additional Readings

Brown, W. C. (1982). College learning assistance: A developmental concept. *Journal of College Student Personnel (September)*, 395-401.

Burns, M. E. (1993). A study to formulate a learning assistance model for the California community college. In S. Mioduski & G. Enright (Eds.). *Proceedings of the 13th and 14th annual institutes for learning assistance professionals.* Tucson: University Learning Center, University of Arizona, 20-23.

Christ, F. L. (1971). Systems for learning assistance: Learners, learning facilitators, and learning centers. In F. L. Christ (Ed.), *Interdisciplinary aspects of reading instruction.* Fourth annual proceedings of the Western College Reading Association, 32-41.

Christ, F. L. (1980). Learning assistance at a state university: A cybernetic model. In K. V. Lauridsen (Ed.), *Examining the scope of learning centers. New directions for college learning assistance.* San Francisco: Jossey-Bass, 45-56.

Clark, E. A. (1980). The learning center in the urban university. In K. V. Lauridsen (Ed.), *Examining the scope of learning centers. New directions for college learning assistance.* San Francisco: Jossey-Bass, 9-17.

Commander, N. E., Stratton, C. B., Callahan, C. A., & Smith, B. D. (1996). A learning assistance model for expanding academic support, *Journal of Developmental Education, 20*, (2), 8-10, 12, 14, 16.

Enright, G. (1995). LAC, LRC, and developmental education: An orientation for the beginning learning center professional. In S. Mioduski & G. Enright (Eds.). *Proceedings of the 15th and 16th annual institutes for learning assistance professionals*, 40-47.

Enright, G., & Kerstiens, G. (1980). The learning center: Toward an expanded role. In O. T. Lenning & R I. Nayman (Eds.). *New roles for learning assistance. New directions for college learning assistance.* San Francisco: Jossey-Bass, 1-24.

Garner, A. (1980). A comprehensive community college model for learning assistance centers. In K.V. Lauridsen (Ed.), *Examining the scope of learning centers. New directions for college learning assistance.* San Francisco: Jossey-Bass, 19-31.

Kerstiens, G. (1972). The ombudsman function of the college learning center. In F. Greene (Ed.), *College reading: Problems and programs of junior and senior colleges.* Twenty-first yearbook of the National Reading Conference, 2, 221-227.

Kerstiens, G. (1995). A taxonomy of learning support services. In S. Mioduski & G. Enright (Eds.). *Proceedings of the 15th and 16th annual institutes for learning assistance professionals*, 48-51.

Lissner, L. S. (1989). College learning assistance programs: The results of a national survey. *Issues in College Learning Centers,* (9), 82-95.

Lissner, L. S. (1990). The learning center from 1829 to the year 2000 and beyond. In R. M. Hashway (Ed.), *Handbook of developmental education*. New York: Praeger Publishers, 127-154.

Martin, D. C., Lorton, M., Blanc, R., & Evans, C. (1978). *The learning center: A comprehensive model for colleges and universities*. Kansas City, MO: Student Learning Center, University of Missouri, ERIC ED 162-294.

Peterson, G. T. (1975). *The learning center: A sphere for nontraditional approaches to education*. Hamden, CT: Shoestring Press.

Smith, K. (1995). Twelve key questions to answer and one critical issue in designing and implementing a collegiate learning center. In S. Mioduski & G. Enright (Eds.). *Proceedings of the 15th and 16th annual institutes for learning assistance professionals*, 54-55.

Walker, C. (1980). The learning assistance center in a selective institution. In K. V. Lauridsen (Ed.), *Examining the scope of learning centers*. San Francisco: Jossey-Bass, 57-68.

Weisberger, R. (1994). Model for the development of an academic support center. In I. Anderson (Ed.), *A sourcebook for developmental educators*. Manchester, NH: Learning Assistance Association of New England, 16-21

Gwyn Enright served as CRLA President in 1987. She had been Editor of the Proceedings from 1978 to 1981 and has published articles on test support programs and on the national status and history of learning assistance in the WCRLA/CRLA Proceedings and the Journal of College Reading and Learning. She received the CRLA Long and Outstanding Service Award in 1996.

QUESTION #2:
HOW CAN I DEVELOP MY PROFESSIONALISM IN LEARNING ASSISTANCE?

A conversation with Karen Smith

By reading extensively in the field and networking with other learning assistance center professionals you will gain immeasurably in professional scholarship.

But why should I consider this important?

To answer that I must first explain why professional involvement is important for me. Our colleagues in higher education immerse themselves in organizations filled with individuals dedicated to the same field, discipline, or activity. They do this for the same reason that we, in learning assistance, seek association with others in learning assistance: in order to learn and become more knowledgeable, to become more skilled in our field, to share our knowledge and skills with others, and to meet colleagues in other colleges and universities. In higher education, professional involvement is considered crucial to advancement and recognition as a dedicated educator, and every new member of the collegiate community is expected to become a member of the professional organization dedicated to his or her discipline or activity.

Without connections to other learning assistance professionals, we can easily become stagnant in our own colleges because we fail to stay current with developments and trends in the field. Isolation from other learning assistance professionals may not only bring about stagnation, but also does not allow others in the field the opportunity to know what we have developed and learned. In addition, our professional credibility is crucial to our image and reputation among our campus colleagues.

How should I begin to find other professionals in my field?

First, join one of the major organizations for learning assistance professionals. The College Reading and Learning Association (CRLA) is the oldest organization dedicated to learning assistance. For me, CRLA has provided the greatest professional growth and connections to peers in our field. In addition, the Midwest College Learning Center Association (MCLCA) and New York College Learning Skills Association (NYCLSA) are organizations focused on learning assistance. Although the National Association for Developmental Education (NADE) is primarily concerned with developmental education, it also includes learning assistance centers in its areas of interest.

If your specialty is in reading education, mathematics or writing, there are other organizations that can help develop your knowledge and skills. The International Reading Association (IRA), the College Reading Association (CRA), the National Council of Teachers of Mathematics (NCTM), the National Council of Teachers of English (NCTE), the Conference on College Composition and Communication (CCCC), and others can provide specialized connections in professional development.

Find out if your state has a local organization for learning assistance professionals. Many do, but if not, call your neighboring community colleges and universities to see if you can locate and connect to other professionals in learning assistance. You will gain much from developing a collegial network to call on for guidance and to answer questions as you develop your program.

Do you have specific recommendations for my reading?

Definitely. A first reading for any new professional in learning assistance is *Improving Student Learning Skills, A New Edition* by Martha Maxwell (1997). Although originally published in 1979, it has been revised and, almost without exception, many learning assistance professionals have read and benefited from its strength.

Read the journals in the field. Read the articles on program description, program development and research on learning assistance in the *Journal of College Reading and Learning* (*JCRL*), published by the College Reading and Learning Association. There are several journals, in addition to *JCRL*, which offer especially relevant information written and researched by your learning assistance colleagues. You will find these especially informative: *Learning Assistance Review* (MCLCA), *Journal of Developmental Education*, *New Directions for Learning Assistance* (Jossey-Bass Publishers), *Reading Research and Instruction* (CRA), *Research and Teaching in Developmental Education* (NYCLSA).

Additional reading can broaden your knowledge about areas that impact on learning assistance and understanding college students and their needs. Casazza and Silverman's

Learning Assistance and Developmental Education (1996) and *Teaching Reading and Study Strategies at the College Level*, edited by Flippo and Caverly (1991), will offer you valuable information. In addition, learn about William Perry, Jr.'s theory on dualism in college learners and read Chickering's books about student development and student life issues, *Education and Identity* and the *Modern American College* (1990). Malcolm Knowles has written extensively on the adult learner and offers a model of human development that differs greatly from that of Piaget. Among several outstanding authors and their work, Richard Paul's writing on critical thinking is pertinent to our work in learning assistance.

By the way, a Research and Scholar's Library for Learning Assistance Professionals is being developed at the University of Missouri in Kansas City. Its catalog will answer all your questions about important reading references.

If I need some stimulation, some new ideas, where can I find them?

Join your colleagues in a national conference. Hear what they have learned and how they are serving students in other LACs. You will find plenty of stimulation and ideas when you network with your colleagues. They've been where you are in the novice's role, and they can help you navigate the collegial waters and miss some of the most treacherous areas. Especially important is that when you attend the conferences or workshops of your choice, you become involved in the organization. Volunteer for committees or workshops or assistance at registration or the exhibits. Let it be known that you are new and want to be actively involved. Then, by all means, follow through and make these new connections into long-term relationships.

I especially enjoy the collegiality and benefits of the CRLA conference, which is held every fall and features hour-long presentations and in-depth institutes on special interest topics, as well as keynote speakers, and a variety of activities devoted to meeting the special interests of every participant. In addition, CRLA's state and regional associations hold conferences and meetings throughout the year and across the country. The MCLCA and NYCLSA conferences are held each fall, as well, and NADE holds conferences in the spring.

Attend the Winter Institute for Learning Assistance Professionals, held every January in Tucson. This institute is a dedicated and intensive week with a knowledgeable group of professionals and mentors in the field and a group of participants like you seeking growth and knowledge.

Watch for announcements about special symposia or conferences in the journals to which you subscribe. Some professional organizations and some colleges and universities arrange special conferences or sessions that may also be beneficial to you.

What can I find about learning assistance centers on the Internet?

Much of the information about organizations and people in learning assistance is available on the Internet. First, subscribe to the listserve for professionals in learning assistance called LRNASST. Introduce yourself to the membership and lurk for awhile, learning about the issues of the day or the year, and then join in the discussions. Ask for assistance for your new program, and others will come to your aid immediately. You'll be amazed at the friends and colleagues who will make themselves available to you.

Next, visit the web site, Learning Support Centers in Higher Education, where you will find a one-stop web site that you can browse to become and stay current in your professional work. It contains a calendar of learning assistance-related events, a directory of associations, lists of resources for professional growth including institutions offering learning assistance related graduate degrees. This is your web site and it will profit from your feedback and input as to its content. Bookmark this URL at (http://www.pvc.maricopa.edu/winterinstitute/).

ADDITIONAL READINGS

Casazza, M. E., & Silverman, S. L. (1996). *Learning assistance and developmental education: A guide for effective practice.* San Francisco: Jossey-Bass.

Caverly, D., & Flippo, R. (1991). *Teaching reading and study strategies at the college level.* International Reading Association.

Chickering, A. (1990). *Education and identity.* San Francisco: Jossey-Bass.

Chickering, A., and others. (1990). *The modern American college.* San Francisco: Jossey-Bass.

Christ, F. L. (1972). Preparing practitioners, counselors, and directors of college learning assistance centers. In F. P. Greene (Ed.), *College reading: Problems and programs of junior and senior colleges.* Twenty-first yearbook of the National Reading Conference, 2, 179-188.

Christ, F. L. (1994). Yesterday's words, tomorrow's challenges. In S. Mioduski & G. Enright (Eds.). *Proceedings of the 13th and 14th annual institutes for learning assistance professionals: 1992 and 1993.* Tucson, AZ: University Learning Center, University of Arizona, 9-11.

Coda-Messerle, M. D. (1980). Professional resources for learning assistance specialists. In K. V. Lauridsen (Ed.), *Examining the scope of learning centers. New directions for college learning assistance.* San Francisco: Jossey-Bass, 87-98.

Garcia, S. (1981). The training of learning assistance practitioners. In F. L. Christ & M. Coda-Messerle (Eds.). *Staff development for learning support systems. New directions for college learning assistance,* 4, 29-37.

Heard, P. (1976). College learning specialists: A profession coming of age. In *Proceedings of the ninth annual conference of the Western College Reading Association*, 1-9.

Knowles, M. (1984). *Andragogy in action*. San Francisco: Jossey-Bass.

Knowles, M. (1988). *The modern practice of adult education*. Cambridge, MA: Cambridge University Press.

Knowles, M. (1998). *The adult learner (4th Ed)*. Gulf Publications.

Matthews, J. M. (1981). Becoming professional in college level learning assistance. In F. Christ & M. Coda-Messerle (Eds.). *Staff development for learning support systems. New directions for college learning assistance*. San Francisco: Jossey Bass, Inc., 1-18.

Maxwell, M. (1981). An annual institute for directors and staff of college learning centers. In F. Christ & M. Coda-Messerle (Eds.). *Staff development for learning support systems. New directions for college learning assistance*. San Francisco: Jossey Bass, Inc., 39-45.

Maxwell, M. (1997). *Improving student learning skills: A new edition*. Clearwater, FL: H&H Publishing Company.

Maxwell, M. (1998). Fellows in learning assistance and developmental education: A proposal. *Journal of College Reading and Learning, 29* (1), 41-47.

Paul, R. (1992). *Critical thinking*. Santa Rosa, CA: Foundation for Critical Thinking.

Karen G. Smith is currently the University Director of the Learning Resource Centers of Rutgers University. She has the distinction of designing, developing and directing learning assistance centers in three unique and different universities: Rutgers University, Tulane University, and New Mexico State University. Karen is a 25-year member of CRLA, a past president (1983-84), NM state director (1975-77), workshop presenter at many conferences, and is currently archivist (1986-) and a member of the JCRL Editorial Board (1997-). One of her proudest achievements is recognition by her peers in CRLA with the Long and Outstanding Service Award. In addition to her commitment to her membership in CRLA, Karen is a long-standing member of IRA and served as the New Mexico State President in 1977. She has consulted widely with other colleges and universities for over 20 years, in learning assistance center design and development, reading education in colleges and universities, and management and supervision in learning centers.

Question #3:
How Do I Answer Faculty Members or Administrators When They Ask Why We Have a Learning Assistance Center on Our Campus?

A conversation with Elaine Burns

You can answer by citing reasons that should satisfy both your faculty and administrators. Administratively the LAC is significant because its programs and services can increase retention rates and certificate completions. Also, when the LAC offers lab courses for credit, captures tutorial hours, and provides a tutor training course, there is an increase in FTE's. A Learning Assistance Center also benefits an institution's recruitment and outreach efforts, is a success component in orientation and probation programs, and a significant campus highlight in school relations and public relations strategies. The LAC can also act as a liaison with neighboring institutions and partner with them, as well as with local businesses.

Those reasons would certainly appeal to my administrators. Are there any other reasons?

Yes, the LAC can establish interrelationships with departments, offices, and services on campus to build the quality and types of services the LAC can offer. For example, two-year institutions could partner with four-year institutions to obtain graduate student assistance, through graduate internships and student teaching programs, for tutorial programs where there are few or no available tutors in upper division courses. The LAC can also work with teachers' retirement groups or a retirement village to obtain additional volunteer tutors.

I can understand that administrators would see the LAC as a significant part of the university but what about faculty?

From a faculty perspective, the LAC is an important campus teaching and learning resource because it can be a place where they can send students for academic skills assistance, for tutorials, for course materials accessible to students outside of the classroom, for testing, and maybe even for improvement of their teaching and computer skills.

Tell me more about student referrals to the LAC.

When faculty refer students to the LAC for basic skills improvement in reading, writing, math, computer literacy, critical thinking, or analytical reasoning, the LAC should use some type of referral form that provides a copy for the student, faculty member and LAC. Such a form would show faculty that the LAC follows through on their referrals.

How else can the LAC be useful for faculty?

There are several ways: in course tutoring by getting faculty involved in both recommending tutors and in training tutors, by being a repository for course syllabi, practice tests, lecture audio or videotapes, and lecture notes, as a testing center for make-up classroom exams, special testing considerations, and proctoring for special exams through telecourses, extension programs, and distance learning programs, and as a center for teaching and learning or as a faculty resource center, with space and equipment for faculty to enhance their knowledge of computers and multimedia, share course outlines, syllabi, and lesson plans. When faculty use the LAC, they will better understand what it is the LAC does on campus and they will promote its use to other faculty and will become advocates for its programs and services.

What particular aspect of the LAC would you emphasize to campus faculty, staff, and administrators?

I would emphasize that the ideal learning assistance center, developed with faculty and administrative support, is a comprehensive support system for everyone: students, faculty, staff, administrators, and community members, not just special populations. Finally, an LAC would offer a wide range of programs and services to students across the curriculum.

Additional Readings

Baker, G., & Painter, P. L. (1983). The learning center: A study of effectiveness. In J. E. Roueche (Ed.), *A new look at successful programs. New directions for college learning assistance.* San Francisco: Jossey-Bass, 73-88.

Beal, P. E. (1980). Learning centers and retention. In O. T. Lenning & D. L. Wayman (Eds.). *New roles for learning assistance. New directions for college learning assistance.* San Francisco: Jossey-Bass, 59-73.

Dempsey, J., & Tomlinson, B. (1980). Learning centers and instructional/curricular reform. In O. T. Lenning & R. T. Nayman (Eds.). *New roles for learning assistance.* San Francisco: Jossey-Bass, 41-58.

Enright, G., & Kerstiens, G. (1980). The learning center: Toward an expanded role. In O. T. Lenning & R. I. Nayman (Eds.). *New roles for learning assistance. New directions for college learning assistance.* San Francisco: Jossey-Bass, 1-24.

Kemig, R. T. (1983). Raising academic standards: A guide to learning improvement. *AAHE/ERIC Education Research Report No. 4.* Washington, D.C.: American Association for Higher Education.

Kerstiens, G. (1972). The ombudsman function of the college learning center. In F. Greene (Ed.), *College reading: Problems and programs of junior and senior colleges.* Twenty-first yearbook of the National Reading Conference, 2, 221-227.

Roueche, S. D. (1983). Elements of program success: Report of a national study. In J. E. Roueche (Ed.), *A new look at successful programs. New directions for college learning assistance.* San Francisco: Jossey-Bass, 3-10.

Smith, K. G., Clymer, C., & Brabham, R. D. (1976). Revolutionizing the attitudes of academia through a learning skills center. In R. Sugimoto (Ed.), *Revolutionizing college learning skills.* Proceedings of the ninth annual conference of the Western College Reading Association, 174-180.

Vincent, V. C. (1983). *Impact of a college learning assistance center on the achievement and retention of disadvantaged students.* ED 283 438.

Dr. Marie-Elaine Burns is the Director of The Learning Center and the Student Support Services - TRIO Program at Skyline College in San Bruno, California. Elaine has directed learning centers for the past nine years and was the Associate Coordinator of the Learning Assistance Support System at California State University, Long Beach under the directorship of Frank Christ for eight years. Her doctoral dissertation is entitled, "A Study to Formulate a Learning Assistance Model for the California Community Colleges." Elaine Burns has a B.A. in Broadcast Communication Arts from San Francisco State University, a M.S. in School Management and Administration and an Ed.D. in Institutional Management, both from Pepperdine University, a California Community College Supervisory Credential, and a California Community College Instructor's Credential in Basic Skills. As President of Mammoth Concepts, her learning assistance consulting company, Dr. Burns conducts learning skills workshops for schools as well as public and private organizations, writes grant proposals for the funding of community learning centers, and provides technical assistance to established community learning centers. She has also published articles on management strategies to assist students in improving their learning skills.

Question #4:
Who Are the Significant Individuals, Units, and Departments That May Support a Campus Learning Assistance Center?

A conversation with Frank Torres

Your question is comprehensive and may take some time to answer. Let me give you the big picture first. I'll talk about individuals, units, and departments that support LAC's at most universities.

First of all, Academic Affairs and Student Affairs are the two most significant divisions at most campuses. Some LACs actually fall under the supervision of Academic Affairs and may be housed in the library, a very significant unit under Academic Affairs. However, the LAC may get its financial support, as we do here at Cal Poly Pomona, both from Academic Affairs through deans, department chairs, and faculty and from Student Affairs directors and staff of programs such as Educational Opportunity Program, Disabled Student Services, Counseling and Psychological Services, and Associated Students.

How do individual faculty support a campus LAC?

Our LAC houses the English department's tutoring program. Some faculty teach English courses to a large number of sections of students who have been placed in those classes because they received low scores on the English Placement Test. Thus, the English instructors who teach English 095 and English 096 appreciate the LAC's tutoring facility and the use of computers which we make available to tutors and tutees.

How do you accommodate so many students?

With great difficulty. We get so crowded in here that many tutors and tutees conduct business on the luxuriant lawn outside or in the large study room next door. Our tutors are versatile. They've been well trained and certified.

What do you mean by certified?

Thanks for asking. All our tutors have to take and pass Level I Certification from CRLA. Our tutor trainer who also is our computer programmer, has presented at CRLA, and he has set up on-line tutor training on our LAC web page, using HTML, Java, C+, and QuickTime captions.

Slow down. Before you get too technical on me, are English instructors the only ones supporting the LAC?

No. We also have a good number of math faculty supporting the LAC. Our math coordinator has a close working relationship with the chair of the math department. They work closely together on developmental math matters. Our LAC offers free math workshops to students who want to retake the Math Diagnostic Test.

Do you work with any other faculty?

Well, each college has a College-Based Program, which targets underrepresented students, and the coordinators of those programs are faculty. Since they work closely with the same type of students we do, they refer students to us and frequently ask LAC to speak to their students about our College Reading Study Skills Program and the free workshops the LAC offers in stress management, time management, critical reading, world wide web, speed reading, and memory improvement.

Now, getting back to faculty who support the LAC. Are there any others?

Well, a large number of faculty from the Colleges of Engineering, Science, and Business refer students to our LAC. Engineering faculty have a significant number of international students who have not mastered English and can't graduate until they pass our institutional Graduate Writing Exam. We provide support for them.

It's clear that you have strong support from Engineering. But what about units from the other colleges? What about science and business faculty and staff, for example?

We have several liaison faculty and staff in the College of Science, Business, Agriculture, and Environmental Design, as many of them are mentors for our federally funded TRIO programs. Our TRIO program assists low-income, first generation college students in the areas of critical reading, critical thinking, vocabulary, reading rate, and writing. The program uses computer software that motivates students to excel. The beauty of this program is that it has generated significant support from senior staff in the departments relevant to Financial Aid, Student Outreach and Recruitment, and the Registrar.

Besides faculty and staff, are there other individuals who support your LAC?

Yes, our president, who has learned about our high school outreach program from discussions with local school superintendents. He was impressed with their favorable remarks about the program and has been a strong LAC supporter ever since.

It really helps to have the president on your side, doesn't it? But I am still interested in knowing about other units or departments at Cal Poly Pomona who also support your LAC.

In addition to Student Affairs, EOP, Disabled Students Services, Athletics, Cultural Centers, Women's Reentry Center, and Psychological Services and Counseling. The best part is that all the units and departments mentioned above have a self-interest in supporting the university's LAC.

Why do you think that?

Because LAC assists thousands of their students each year. We help to retain and graduate their students. We also succeed in placing many of them into graduate school.

I see. You work in collaboration with them. So, if their students or clients need academic help, they refer them to you.

Exactly. I have discovered that strong personal relationships with faculty, staff, and student-centered units and departments across campus pay off in many ways. They support the LAC because that means that they support their students. They support my grant proposals because those proposals are student centered. And they support many of my requests for expansion of my programs because I share the outcomes of my LAC programs with them in the form of a Year End Report. In fact, a good percentage of the financing for LAC programs and student assistance came from telephone calls that I received from my friends throughout campus. In turn, they can depend on me to deliver excellent academic support for the students they refer to LAC. These successes and interpersonal relationships are a source of great satisfaction for all of my staff and myself.

ADDITIONAL READINGS

Burns-Reed, M. E., & Dozen, P. (1982). New partnerships in academe. In H. Boylan (Ed.), *Forging new partnerships in learning assistance. New directions for college learning assistance.* San Francisco: Jossey-Bass, 17-29.

Knight, B., & Helm, P. (1981). Developing trustee commitment to learning assistance. In F. Christ & M. Coda-Messerle (Eds.). *Staff development for learning support systems. New directions for college learning assistance.* San Francisco: Jossey Bass, 19-27.

Frank Torres has been involved in learning assistance since 1972. He is the founding director of the Learning Resource Center (1972 - present) at California State Polytechnic University, Pomona (Cal Poly Pomona). His professional interests in student persistence and graduation at the college level led to the writing and awarding of four TRIO projects (Student Support Services, Upward Bound Classic, Upward Bound Math & Science, and McNair Scholars) from the U.S. Department of Education. In addition to directing the LRC and TRIO projects, Frank is a tenured professor of English at his campus where he recruits staff and faculty as advisors, coordinators, and directors of the seven programs within the LRC. He is involved in the broader community where he serves as a trustee of the Los Angeles Educational Alliance For Restructuring Now (LEARN). He also serves as a leader with the Industrial Areas Foundation (IAF) which is currently reorganizing clusters of institutions, religious groups, political allies, and community leaders to form a robust political entity in the greater Los Angeles metropolitan area. Frank has been a member of CRLA since 1971.

QUESTION #5:
HOW DO I SUPPORT DIFFERENT EXPECTATIONS OF ADMINISTRATION, DEPARTMENTS, FACULTY, STUDENTS, AND SPECIAL UNITS?

A conversation with Sylvia Mioduski

Directing a Learning Assistance Center requires many talents. At the very least you are expected to be a visionary, a manager, a coordinator, an instructor, a budget analyst, a counselor, an advisor, sometimes, even a clairvoyant. Everyone has an idea about how you should run the LAC, what it should offer, and what students should be expected to accomplish. Before you focus on others' expectations, be sure you are clear about your own expectations. What is the primary mission of your unit? What do you hope to accomplish? Why? Armed with this information, you can then begin to get to "know your audience." Who are the individuals and the groups who have a stake in the LAC on your campus? What are their expectations? Why do they view the LAC as they do? You will need to be able to answer these questions in order to both support their varying expectations while, at the same time, maintaining credibility with and for the students you serve.

One of the first steps you must take is to commit time for learning about your campus community. A tactical error many of us in learning support programs make is deciding that we must focus 100% of our time on service delivery and dismissing as "I just don't have time" the need to read, plan, and think about where we're headed and why. This is something that you must do whether you are new to your position or a seasoned veteran. When you "do your homework" and know the key factors about your campus, its culture, and its future direction, it allows you to formulate questions and strategize more effectively. Familiarize yourself with the mission statement and the strategic plan for your institution. How does your unit fit? What questions does it raise that you might want to pursue with your administrators? What do various groups think about the LAC? Are they supportive? Do they view it as strictly remedial? Do they see it as a resource for all students or only certain groups of students? Do they see it as a resource for faculty and staff? What is the history of the LAC on your campus?

What do you think drives these expectations?

Oh, a multitude of factors! It might be political. Perhaps there are issues related to business/industry. Financial implications— available budget and the demand for services —are often a major factor. Sometimes expectations are driven by personal experience, either one's own or that of constituents who tell us about their experience. It could be the division your unit sits in. Student Affairs and Academic Affairs each have their own distinct culture and ways of doing business. And make it a point to understand the relationship between the institution and your state legislature. How your lawmakers view higher education and the state's role in funding or creating and implementing policy can have a major impact on the LAC.

How do I get this information?

Ask! Set up individual meetings, attend staff/faculty meetings, use surveys, and visit with student groups.

How do I know whom I really need to meet? And how do I orchestrate these meetings?

My personal bias is that you ultimately want to meet as many administrators, faculty, program directors, staff, and representatives from student leadership as you can. And you want to involve as many of your staff as possible and appropriate. Begin by making a list of the key players. Here are some examples.

Your President. You really need to understand this individual's vision for your institution and the way that vision relates to students. Read examples of key reports, presentations to your governing board, faculty senate, community leaders, etc. If your President has a homepage, visit it regularly. This is someone you eventually need to meet. Depending on the size of your campus and/or the availability of time in his/her schedule, getting an appointment may take a while. But, get an appointment or invite him/her to the center!

Your Provost. Many campuses have an individual who is the chief academic officer or provost. This person is charged with providing direction and guidance for the institution's academic programs. The LAC is charged with providing academic support whether the unit reports organizationally in Academic Affairs or Student Affairs. It will be important for you to know what the Provost believes about academic support programs because he is a direct link to the College Deans.

College Deans. This is a vastly underrated group of administrators, in my opinion. We consider them to be very busy and truly uninterested in the work that we do. But on many campuses, individual colleges are a forceful presence. This underscores, again, the importance of understanding your campus culture and campus politics. Deans are often in a position to advocate on behalf of the LAC, particularly regarding budget and space. If they know who you are and how the LAC helps their students—retention and persistence are important terms to incorporate into discussions with them—they will be more inclined to offer support.

Campus Faculty. Faculty can be among your strongest allies in encouraging students to utilize the LAC. And they are an excellent resource in marketing the LAC to other faculty. A growing number of centers are using a faculty liaison model similar to the one developed at Paradise Valley Community College in Phoenix, AZ. Faculty liaisons facilitate two-way communication between the LAC and departments external to it. Among their responsibilities are providing information about the LAC to peers and in department/division/college meetings, looking at instructional support issues for students regarding LAC services, and providing input and feedback regarding new LAC policies and procedures. In this model, faculty becomes an integral part of the LAC staff.

Directors of Other Campus Programs. These individuals have a variety of titles including Assistant Dean, Director, Associate/Assistant Director, Coordinator, etc. They are responsible for directing programs/services such as athletics, disability services, residence life, Student Support Services, Honors, multicultural offices, technology centers, grants offices, Freshman Year Experience programs, Orientation, etc. They are often your peers, the ones you will interact with on a regular basis. Talk with them about their experience with the LAC, existing collaborations, or the potential for new ones. Identify the resources you might collectively share.

Campus Staff. If faculty are among the strongest allies, staff are positioned right next to them! Remember that staff members are often the ones who have the most frequent and on-going contact with students. They are the ones who likely do many of the referrals to the LAC so it is critical that their information is accurate and up-to-date. Offer to meet with them individually or attend one of their staff meetings, or do a short presentation on a key learning assistance strategy. Frank Christ suggests that everyone needs time management!

And, of course, students. What are the needs of the students you serve? How do you know this? If you are grant funded, you will need to become very familiar with the criteria approved for selecting participants. If you are institutionally funded, criteria may have already been established. Or you may have an opportunity to set the criteria. Also, find out about student leadership opportunities on your campus and then create opportunities to learn about their needs. Again, participating in their meetings, scheduling separate time to meet with them, offering workshops on topics of interest to the group are ways to learn more about the students and to engender their support for the LAC.

These meetings will certainly give me a wealth of information. But, how do I balance everyone's needs and expectations?

Again, go back to the mission of your institution. Whether your LAC is funded by the institution or by a grant, whatever you do has to fit within that framework. You want to insure that you maintain credibility with your students. That means quality and consistency in service delivery, that service is available when you say it will be, and that students are treated equitably.

Are there certain times of the year or semester when I should make contacts?

This is a good point. You need an annual plan. Whom do you need to visit annually? Each semester or quarter? Whom, in addition to your staff, do you need to meet with regularly throughout the year? Depending on the size of your campus and the breadth of your services, are there some groups that you might cycle through every 2-3 semesters?

Is it better to hold these meetings at the LAC or in individuals' offices?

Whenever possible, get people into your center. Remember that most of us retain a much greater percentage of the information we can see and feel. Let them see where tutoring happens, experience the actual environment you have created. It is always useful to have administrators see a live demonstration of the ways in which you have expended the allocated funds! However, you also want to be sensitive to the needs of the individuals you meet with. Time or circumstances may dictate a variety of meeting locales.

Your advice is sound and I really appreciate it but it sounds, well . . . overwhelming. How am I going to do all of this?

One day at a time! Remember, you are going to need time to structure a plan of action with appropriate timelines. Those of us who have been working in the field for a number of years didn't start with everything in place. As a matter of fact, some of us—myself included—learned many of these lessons by trial and error. Use resources including many of the references included in this monograph. More important, perhaps, is knowing that the contributors of these conversations are real people who have experience similar to yours and that they are still active as mentors and resources who are available to you. Know that you do not have to be alone in this process!

Additional Readings

Martin, D. C., & Blanc, R. (1980). The learning center's role in retention: Integrating student support services with departmental instruction. *Journal of Developmental & Remedial Education*, (4), 2-4.

Shaw, G. (1994). Multiple dimensions of academic support: One learning center's response to learning diversity. In R. Lemelin (Ed.), *Issues in access to higher education*. Portland, ME: University of Southern Maine, 14-16.

Xenakis, F. S. (1979). Learning assistance support system for disadvantaged nursing students. In G. Enright (Ed.), *Multicultural diversity and learning*. Twelfth annual proceedings of the Western College Reading Association, Vol. XII, Los Angeles, 128-132.

Sylvia Mioduski, a member of CRLA for most of her professional career, completed a two-year term as national treasurer in November 1998. Currently, she is the coordinating representative for Arizona CRLA. Sylvia is the director of the University Learning Center and the Freshman Year Center at the University of Arizona. Along with Frank Christ and Rick Sheets, she also co-directs the annual Winter Institute for Learning Assistance Directors and Practitioners.

QUESTION #6:
WHAT IS THE ROLE OF THE LAC WITH SPECIAL POPULATIONS?

A conversation with Sylvia Mioduski

The Learning Assistance Center's role is to be the one "safe" place on a campus where students can turn for help to fulfill their dream of going to college. For some, it is a dream that begins very young. For some, the dream is born in high school. And for some, the dream comes from someone else who sees the potential and nurtures the possibilities. However it happens that individuals become college students, the reality is often unnerving. The student is in a new—dare I say "foreign"—environment responding to new sets of expectations for academic performance, personal growth, and social interaction. College is a culture that expects students to know what to do and how to do it with minimal guidance and direction, a culture that perpetuates the myth many students believe: "I should be able to do this on my own."

We know the range of issues that impact a student's ability to successfully navigate the college experience: developing academic and intellectual competence; establishing and maintaining interpersonal relationships; developing personal identity; deciding on a career and lifestyle; maintaining personal health and wellness; and developing an integrated philosophy. As I said earlier, the LAC is frequently the one "safe" place on a campus where students can turn for help.

Why do you think students see the LAC as such a "safe" resource?

It is, in my opinion, the people who work in the LAC that make the difference. Students gravitate towards individuals who are willing to listen, assist, and provide quality referrals. They look for resources that will help. They look for a place to belong that does not judge them for what they "should" know but do not.

On the other hand, many students believe they are prepared but, in fact, are not. They are not prepared for the level of commitment, the intensity of the reading and writing assignments, the need to learn to navigate a completely new system. Many are living on their own for the first time. First-generation college students do not have role models at home that have experienced the college environment.

Students with learning or physical disabilities have additional needs such as determining the physical accessibility of university buildings, finding notetakers, readers or signers, making arrangements for books on tape or extended time for testing. The LAC may be the designated department on a campus for these students or it may be the resource students turn to for referral.

I understand the students' issues, but how does a Learning Assistance Center create the environment that attracts students?

I'd like to respond to this question with an example. One of the greatest professional experiences I had was the opportunity to work with the Office of Minority Student Affairs, OMSA, at the University of Arizona. In the early 1980's, the university made the decision to support increasing recruitment and retention of ethnic minority and low-income students and established OMSA for this purpose. The Office was staffed with a team of outstanding professionals with a common vision: create a welcoming environment that would encourage students to enroll, persist, and graduate. This included developing a recruitment office, a tutoring program in math and science, expanding an already successful summer bridge program, and implementing a first year program.

As you can imagine, this was a labor-intensive endeavor. The team had a limited number of full-time staff and a minimal budget. The decision was made to increase the staff by utilizing university undergraduate and graduate students as peer recruiters, peer counselors, and peer tutors and by turning to the academic departments for graduate teaching assistants for courses. In addition, there was a conscious decision to enhance the environment of OMSA by recruiting both student and professional staff who represented the students we wanted to recruit and retain.

Extensive use of peers ultimately resulted in a 10% increase in minority student enrollment. In addition, research conducted in 1993 by the Testing Office concluded that students who were involved in multiple programs sponsored by OMSA were retained at a rate 8% higher than a cohort who was not involved. This retention figure also supported the idea that community is created not just by one experience but through many experiences.

Are you suggesting that I look at certain things to create the right environment?

Absolutely. Although my example described a learning assistance center for a specific population, there are specifics any LAC must address. These include a focus on a quality process in staff recruitment, hiring, supervision, training, advocacy and involvement.

Would you talk some more about recruitment and hiring?

Be clear about the criteria you set for the positions in the LAC. Market your positions as widely as possible and also target those populations represented in your LAC. Do you serve students with disabilities? Students from underrepresented populations? Students who are academically at-risk? New traditional students, age 25-30? Veterans? Whether you are recruiting professional staff, graduate students or undergraduate peers, look for individuals who not only meet the criteria of the position but also serve as role models for your students. Also, make it a point to involve the faculty in assisting with the recruitment process. They see the students in their classes and are in a position to encourage applications from students who might not see themselves as potential candidates.

How important is staff supervision?

Providing feedback to staff on a continuous basis is a requisite for a quality program. Regularly scheduled staff meetings provide the opportunity for updating training and for regular review of policies, procedures, and issues. I believe it is important that all staff be involved in this opportunity whether they are faculty, professional, or peer staff. It is important for everyone to remember that they work for their department and have responsibilities to it.

How do you train your staff?

Training involves more than an overview of services. Excellent training programs include detailed information, role-play, and the opportunity for trainees to provide feedback to let you know how well they understand the material. It provides a unique environment to demonstrate what we know about how people learn through a variety of modalities. And it creates the opportunity to demonstrate effective utilization of today's technology that supports extending and expanding training beyond the traditional workday. Through listservs, regular email, websites, tools such as WebBoard, training can continue on any given day and at an hour that best suits the trainee.

Earlier, you mentioned involvement. How do you get yourself and your staff involved with students?

My staff and I use many approaches to demonstrating the LAC's interest in its students. We seem to be most successful by getting involved with students outside the LAC. We go to classrooms, the cafeteria, the residence halls, any place where students congregate. Then, as we have gained the confidence of our students, they have extended invitations to us to participate in their class and club events both on and off campus. It is important that you make the time to be present at some of these occasions.

Earlier, you also used the term, advocacy. What did you mean by that?

Prepare yourself well to be an advocate for your students. For example, know the basics about your institutional policies and procedures that guide your students' progress toward their degree, the federal and state laws that impact your students and the institution, like the Americans with Disabilities Act, Section 504 of the 1973 Vocational Rehabilitation Act, and the financial aid rules.

Wait a minute! I've been hired to work in the LAC. I'm not the financial aid office and I'm not designated as the ADA compliance officer. You mean I really need to know all of these rules?

I understand that it may seem overwhelming. But this is also why it is so important to know your institution's position about your students. There will be times when you may be the *only* advocate for your students. It may be that the institution considers *you* the expert on some of these issues whether your LAC has direct responsibility or not. Remember the old adage: Knowledge is Power. If you know how to access information you are in a much stronger position to be a powerful advocate.

Point well taken! With all that you've suggested, is there a preferred way to begin?

Although every institution, every LAC, and every campus responsibility is different, consider how you can incorporate some of the ideas we discussed here. Whatever you do, trust your instinct in your work with your students. Talk to them. Seek their input. Listen to their message. Although their verbal communication will give you information, it is often their unexpressed message that speaks volumes. Listening to students is the most important skill that LAC administrators and their staff bring to their work with students, especially with special campus populations.

ADDITIONAL READINGS

Martin, D. C. & Blanc, R. (1980). The learning center's role in retention: Integrating student support services with departmental instruction. *Journal of Developmental & Remedial Education*, (4), 2-4.

Pflug, R. J. (1973). The handicapped and disadvantaged students in the learning center. In G. Kerstiens (Ed.), *Technological alternatives in learning*. Proceedings of the sixth annual conference of the Western College Reading Association, 131-135.

Shaw, G. (1994). Multiple dimensions of academic support: One learning center's response to learning diversity. In R. Lemelin (Ed.), *Issues in access to higher education*. Portland, ME: University of Southern Maine, 14-16.

Xenakis, F. S. (1979). Learning assistance support system for disadvantaged nursing students. In G. Enright (Ed.), *Multicultural diversity and learning*. Twelfth annual proceedings of the Western College ReadingAssociation, Los Angeles, 128-132.

Sylvia Mioduski, a member of CRLA for most of her professional career, completed a two-year term as national treasurer in November 1998. Currently, she is the coordinating representative for Arizona CRLA. Sylvia is the director of the University Learning Center and the Freshman Year Center at the University of Arizona. Along with Frank Christ and Rick Sheets, she also co-directs the annual Winter Institute for Learning Assistance Directors and Practitioners.

Question #7:
What Is the Role of Faculty in the Development and Operation of LAC Programs and Services?

A conversation with Michael F. O'Hear

Basically, there are three types of faculty on most campuses: one, those who believe learning centers deal only with students of modest ability who take the place of more "deserving" students and who will probably fail even with help from the center; two, those who support the concept of learning centers, but have little idea of what goes on there; and three, those who are active advocates willing to help if approached at the right time in the right way. The ideal is to activate the third group, fold the second group into the third, and wear down the first. Getting faculty involved with the center has three phases: creating the climate; offering low risk opportunities, and gaining major active support for the center.

The first major element in developing faculty support and assistance is creating the climate, which involves getting the word out on the LAC, its staff, activities, and students. Frequent reports featuring programs, number and type of students served, staff achievements, and testimonials from students, create the idea that the center is active and making a difference. In the beginning stages of my program, I made such reports monthly. Now that the program is established, reports come out twice a year. I use the school's news organ for happenings that occur between the two reports.

On a large campus, I've found that attending department meetings to explain the LAC program both serves to inform and helps to associate a human face with the program, a most important success factor. People who know who I am and what the center does will be more likely to support programs and recommend them to their students. I also use these occasions to indicate how much I value faculty input in developing programs. I offer faculty a selection of low risk possibilities for direct and indirect support. For example, I tell them that our LAC staff will be willing to come to their classes to offer specialized study skill programs and promise them feedback on referrals, if they wish it and if the students approve doing so. Many feel this is an important item because they have no other way of knowing whether the students they send to the LAC ever arrive there.

It would seem almost impossible to get to all faculty on a large campus. How do you do this?

Since there are so many departments on a large campus, I found it necessary to target meetings only of those which offered the best opportunity for working relationships. On my campus, this included Chemistry, English, Education, Math, Nursing, Psychology, and Sociology.

In approaching faculty, a positive attitude is essential. We know that they are concerned and that we can help them do their jobs more effectively. Even when they have off-the-wall ideas, we are willing to discuss them. Since we can't get all faculty involved in the LAC, it is a good idea to locate a small, select group whom we can get involved and who may be able to influence their departments. In doing so, notice who asks questions at department meetings, look for those whose body language indicates interest and buttonhole individual faculty from departments visited to discuss LAC programs. From those who seem most interested, select the core group. Although all faculty may be invited to participate in LAC programs, this initial cadre is singled out for special invitations. These are people to stay in touch with constantly. This special group may be asked to publicize programs in their classes and invited to meetings with selected student groups.

To encourage greater faculty participation in LAC programs, it is important to get them into the facilities. An open house with free coffee and cookies draws certain faculty supporters to the center. Frequently these people bring friends who then gain a first exposure to the LAC.

Earlier, you used the term "low risk opportunities." What do you mean by that?

I always believe in starting with low risk requests in working with faculty. One simple, but potentially valuable contribution is allowing a class to be videotaped for use with students in developing notetaking skills. I have also found faculty willing to tape brief discussions of their department's introductory course content, which can be placed in the center for student reference along with a course syllabus. Provision of copies of tests for use with students is another quick and valuable addition to LAC materials. Once faculty start using this procedure, they continue to do so. Whenever students experience problems, they are sent to the LAC for help with copies of their tests. This procedure has proven so effective in improving student grades in one department that its instructors are constantly proclaiming the LAC's success across campus.

Do you have an advisory board or committee for your LAC?

Yes, we do. And, it seems to me that a higher level of commitment is required from faculty in agreeing to serve on the LAC advisory committee. If well-chosen, this group can provide valuable input and increase faculty support for the LAC. If people chosen are well-respected on campus, they can articulate LAC needs with important campus committees and with the central administration. This is particularly significant when budget issues are involved. While administrators don't necessarily listen to faculty appeals, they will be much more likely to respond to them than to requests from the LAC director presented without active faculty support.

Even when the LAC advisory committee is mandated with membership determined by faculty vote as it is on my campus, lobbying potential candidates may influence them to run for open positions. Since my committee also has *ex officio* appointments from the math and English departments, I have found that discussing these appointments with the chairs has resulted in choices favorable to the LAC program.

What are some other ways to involve faculty with the LAC?

Another way to meet and interest faculty in the LAC is service on campus committees. When faculty see LAC staff frequently in meetings, they not only put a human face to the LAC, but may begin to use the few minutes before a meeting, or the walk across campus to the meeting place, as opportunities to discuss their concerns about student success. This also gives time to tell these new friends about the LAC and to solicit their involvement in center programs.

I have found another way to involve faculty in helping the LAC while helping themselves as well. There have been times when research opportunities have allowed collaboration with junior faculty who need as much research as they can get to attain tenure. On my campus, investigations of sociology textbooks and student behaviors in developmental math have resulted in an increase of knowledge about study situations (a benefit for LAC staff) and publications/presentations that have helped the faculty members' tenure cases both in the areas of teaching and research. Such efforts solidify relationships and garner support for the LAC. A further benefit is that research presented or published with an LAC staff member's name on it increases identification of the LAC with faculty interests. The fact that I do research makes faculty mentally separate me from non-academic staff and lends a credibility to the LAC not easily obtained otherwise.

Once faculty are willing to support the LAC, Supplemental Instruction (SI) and tutoring provide special opportunities for meaningful collaboration. Although there may be some faculty who would not participate in SI, I have not found them. SI is a great opportunity for faculty to make a difference to students and to make their own lot easier with minimal risk to themselves. Who would not want better students in class? And all the faculty member needs to do is encourage people to participate, allow the SI leader to sit in class, and provide occasional materials and feedback to the leader. Recommending tutors gives faculty added confidence in the quality of those providing services to their students. While involving faculty in tutor certification is more difficult to arrange because it requires a greater time commitment, the argument that the process benefits their students combined with positive results they've experienced will carry the day with some faculty. Limited success is all that is normally possible here because so many faculty, even supportive ones, will list extensive demands on their time as reason for non-involvement.

Are there some problems for the LAC when faculty get involved?

Yes, LAC involvement in faculty development provides great opportunities, but requires some initial caution. Faculty are frequently reluctant to undergo training under non-faculty personnel. I have found two approaches that work. First is participation in the campus effective teaching group. This organization is interested in sponsoring sessions on successful instructional methods and on campus agencies that can help faculty do their jobs more effectively. This was a natural fit because a sponsored session was sure to get many faculty to a meeting where they were introduced to the LAC and its staff. In fact, we always have at least one staff member, and sometimes several, at all activities aimed at improving teaching. Our presence and participation in group sessions reinforces the idea that we are primarily interested in academic effectiveness. This in turn adds to faculty support for the LAC.

Sometimes, departments have their own effective teaching groups, which are eager for presentations meaningful to their faculty. For example, our English Department runs round table discussions for new and associate faculty. This is a great forum for introducing people from a critical department to the LAC and for soliciting their involvement in its programs.

A second effective approach has been offering the LAC facilities to faculty for running occasional class sessions. We have had faculty from business, communications, education, English, math, nursing, and psychology use our computer rooms for class sessions and for testing. Nursing works with our LAC to put an important math test on our computers and to schedule their students to take it. Chemistry and math have run study sessions in the LAC and used its computers to house important software for their introductory courses. In both cases, students were assured that work with the software would enhance grades. In most cases, these assurances were accurate.

Success becomes the great builder of relationships and active support. We recognize faculty participation in LAC activities and trumpet their efforts to the entire campus. When they support the LAC, everyone knows.

When LAC programs succeed, everyone knows. Faculty involvement with the LAC is a win-win situation. The more faculty who experience this, the greater the level of support. No, not everyone will ever think the LAC is worthwhile or take advantage of its services, but the numbers who do so are constantly increasing.

Additional Readings

Lowenstein, S. (1993). Using advisory boards for learning assistance programs. In *Perspectives on Practice in Developmental Education*. New York College Learning Skills Association.

Shaw, J. (1980). Learning centers and the faculty: Improving academic competency. In O.T. Lenning & R. Nayman (Eds.). *New roles for learning assistance. New directions for college learning assistance*, (2), 25-39.

Michael F. O'Hear has been a member of CRLA since 1976 and is currently serving as CRLA's President. Mike served as an editor on the WCRLA Proceedings for several years. He was the initial editor of the WCRA Journal, the forerunner of today's JOURNAL OF COLLEGE READING AND LEARNING. A long-time editorial board member for JCRL, Mike served for two years as its editor in the mid-80's. A frequent contributor to developmental education journals, Mike has received two distinguished research awards from CRLA and won its research assistance award in 1994. Mike has headed the Transitional Studies program at Indiana University–Purdue University, Fort Wayne since 1976. An associate professor of English and Linguistics, he has been an assistant dean of Arts and Sciences since 1990.

Question #8:
What Management Tools May Be Useful for the Success of LAC Programs and Services?

A conversation with David Gerkin

I prefer to use the term Learning Support Center or LSC in place of LAC. My campus just changed its name to be in line with national trends and to be more descriptive for students.

The question implies that there is a manager of the LSC. I prefer to think of the person with ultimate responsibility for the LSC, regardless of title, as a leader rather than a manager, a leader of people rather than a manager of a department; this puts the focus on people who are your most valuable resource and the reason for the existence of the LSC.

All right then, to use your terminology, what leadership tools would be useful for the success of LSC programs and services?

One of the most effective leadership tools for many is the mission statement. I would suggest that you, as a leader of the center, begin with writing a personal mission statement. This will connect you to your personal values which can than lead you to reflecting on how these relate to the values of your LSC. This is where your staff come in. Ask each staff member to write a personal mission statement; then come together as a group to discuss LSC values and how they relate to each staff member's personal values. This process culminates in the creation of a mission statement for your center. Since it was written by the entire staff and flows out of personal values, each staff member will have buy-in and feel a sense of ownership for the statement and for the center.

Your LSC mission statement can then be used by you and your staff to help you keep on track; and to reflect on it periodically to answer the question: "Are we doing what we said is important to us?" It is also helpful as a starting point for writing goals, objectives and activities. Another effective use of your mission statement is to put it in your publicity materials to let others know what your LSC stands for.

You seem to be suggesting that staff plays an important role in the leadership of the LSC, but I am the manager or leader. What roles does my staff play in leading the center?

The staff of your LSC can play a crucial role in the leadership of the center. I suggest that you, as a leader, do everything you can to develop the leadership ability of every one of your staff. The leader who is not afraid to hire staff who are smarter than he or she is and who encourages and supports the staff's professional and personal development will be rewarded with a vital, successful, organization with dedicated, highly competent staff who work hard to achieve the goals of the center.

You mentioned goals, objectives, and activities, earlier. How do I use these effectively to run my center?

Virtually all management or leadership methods deal with goals and objectives in some form. I would suggest three keys to using them effectively. First, the entire staff must agree to the goals of the center so that all will work together enthusiastically to achieve the goals. Empower your staff to collaborate with you on the goals and objectives of the center. This must involve a genuine openness to staff ideas on your part; you must be looking for more than agreement with what you propose. If your goals and objectives flow from a mission statement created by your staff team which embodies shared values, you will have staff buy-in.

A second key to utilizing goals and objectives effectively is to monitor progress toward achievement, reflect on the processes involved, and revise the processes or the goals themselves as needed. Finally, it is important to celebrate your team's success when goals are achieved.

You have talked quite a bit about collaborating with staff and working together as a team. This sounds nice; but frankly, some staff can be difficult to work with. How can I collaborate with a staff member to whom I have trouble relating to or getting along with?

I suggest researching several behavioral style instruments and using one or more with your staff to promote understanding of differences in behavioral, personality, work, and learning styles. This can enable you to work well with and appreciate the talents of staff members who are very different from you and with whom you may find yourself often coming into conflict.

Here are three instruments I recommend: 1) the Personal Profile System: DiSC, which categorizes behavioral styles in four categories— dominance, influence, conscientiousness, and steadiness, rating each person's level of behavioral tendency for each category; (2) the Myers-Briggs Type Indicator (MBTI), which assesses preferences for four ways of relating to the environment: where you direct your energy, how you acquire information, how you make decisions, and how you deal with the outer world; and (3) the Learning Type Measure (LTM), which indicates four preferred modes of learning—innovative, analytical, common sense, and dynamic—and incorporates right and left brain modalities as well.

Regardless of which instrument or instruments you use, I suggest you and each staff member complete it and discuss the results as a group. You will most likely discover that you can capitalize on each other's strengths, compensate for and improve in weak areas, work better as a team, and learn to go beyond appreciation to celebration of differences.

There is so much to do when running a center, it seems that time management tools would be important. Which tools do you suggest?

There are many time management systems and methods available. I suggest trying several and discovering which works best for you. It may be a combination or modification of systems or approaches that is most effective for you. There are two approaches I would recommend as starting points.

The first is Stephen Covey's idea that you must know what is important to you before you can decide how to most effectively spend your time. Therefore, he emphasizes personal mission as a prerequisite to time management. The second approach is Carlson and Bailey's suggestion that we must recognize our thought processes which tend to speed up our thinking and cause us to feel hurried and stressed. If we recognize these hurried, overly analytical thoughts, we can release them and free our minds to work in a more effective, less stressful, free flowing mode.

You seem to be suggesting management approaches that begin with thinking and learning about myself. Are there any tools for this reflective approach?

I'm glad you asked that! Reflective journaling is an excellent strategy for reflecting on your values, mission, goals, behavioral styles, effectiveness, interpersonal communication skills, in fact, any thoughts and feelings about your work life.

Periodic reflective journaling, daily, weekly, or bi-weekly, allows you to slow down and think about what you have been so busy about. It creates the needed time and space to reflect on, evaluate, and gain insight into the processes and interactions of your daily work. Another way to practice reflection is to build it into staff meetings and retreats. Brief reviews and discussions of mission, goals, objectives, progress, or conflicts can be placed on the agenda for weekly or monthly staff meetings. More in-depth reflective exercises such as journaling, structured discussion, and group brainstorming of accomplishments and challenges can be undertaken at department retreats.

You mention staff meetings. Are there some techniques that can make my staff meetings more effective?

Two techniques I have found to be effective for staff meetings come from the field of Total Quality Management (TQM). The first is to come to agreement, as a group, on a set of "Ground Rules" or guidelines for behavior at the meeting. These often deal with topics such as respectful communication, confidentiality, and the tone of the meeting. The second technique is the "Issue Bin." Items of discussion or ideas that occur during the meeting that may take the meeting off track or that can not be dealt with in the time allotted are written on a flip chart designated as the "Issue Bin." These issues are recognized as important and are captured to be dealt with at a more appropriate time.

ADDITIONAL READINGS

Burns, J. M. (1978). *Leadership*. New York: Harper and Row Publishers.

Burns, M. E. (1986). Management strategies to assist students in improving learning skills. *Journal of Developmental Education,* (9), 3, 2-4.

Burns, M. E. (1987). *Leadership styles and management skills of learning assistance/developmental education program directors/coordinators*. ERIC ED288472.

Carlson, R., & Bailey, J. (1997). *Slowing down to the speed of life*. New York: Harper Collins.

Christ, F. L. (1977). Management of a learning assistance sector. In G. Enright (Ed.), *Personalizing learning systems: Ecologies and strategies*. Tenth annual proceedings of the Western College Reading Association, 76-84.

Christ, F. L. (1997). Using MBO to create, develop, improve, and sustain learning assistance programs. In S. Mioduski & G. Enright (Eds.). *Proceedings of the 17th and 18th annual institutes for learning assistance professionals*, 43-51.

Covey, S. R. (1992). *Principle centered leadership*. New York: Summit Books.

Covey, S. R. (1994). *First things first.* New York: Simon and Shuster, 103-117.

Jones, L. B. (1996). *The path: Creating your mission statement for work and for life.* New York: Hyperion.

Milesko-Pytelin (1994). Total quality management in college learning centers. *Research & Teaching in Developmental Education, 11,* 1, 115-123.

Sheets, R. A. (1997). 5 C's of learning assistance center director as manager: Compassion, commitment, connections, credibility, catalyst. In S. Mioduski and G. Enright (Eds.). *Proceedings of the 17th and 18th annual institutes for learning assistance professionals,* 82-84.

Sherr, L. A., & Teeter, D. J. (1991). *Total quality management in higher education.* San Francisco: Jossey-Bass.

David M. Gerkin was born in Fitchburg, Massachusetts on November 15, 1956 and has resided in Phoenix, Arizona since 1963. He received his elementary education in Fitchburg and Phoenix and graduated from Moon Valley High School in 1974. He received an Associate of Arts degree in 1990 from Scottsdale Community College and an Associate of General Studies degree with high honors from Paradise Valley Community College in 1991. Mr. Gerkin began attending Ottawa University in the fall of 1992 and graduated with a Bachelor of Arts degree with a major in Adult Education in 1994. He received his Master of Arts in Counseling from Ottawa University in 1995. He received the Professional Staff Employee of the Year Award in 1993 from Paradise Valley Community College when he was employed as a Learning Technician in the Learning Assistance Center. Mr. Gerkin currently holds the position of Director of the Learning Support Center at Paradise Valley Community College. His professional areas of interest include tutor training, learning styles, study strategies, leadership development, and the transformation of post-secondary institutions into learning centered organizations. He is a guitar player, singer, and songwriter and enjoys spending time with his wife Aimée, his two teenage sons, Kyle and Noah, and his newborn son, Samuel.

Question #9:
How Can Technology Enhance the Programs and Services of the Learning Assistance Center?

A conversation with Rick Sheets

Let me start by defining technology as more than computers, though most recent advances in technology usually incorporate computers or computer chips. Technology involves the application of science as a tool. Technology can include the use of videotape players, calculators, computers, data projectors, video or audio enhancing devices, or other types of equipment. Using the definition of technology as a tool, appropriate technology can thus enhance many aspects of a program or service. Some of the major technology areas that typically enhance our LAC programs and services include office and program management, instructional support, presentations and communication. Technology also provides new options for remote access to programs and services locally and globally.

Can you give some examples?

Yes. Office and program management aspects include using databases to schedule students with tutors, maintain staff and tutoring records, track training, and monitor time worked; using word processing for handouts, brochures, reports, and forms; and using spreadsheets or online systems to approve, track, and record budget transactions and also to maintain charts and long-term trend data for reports, use statistics, and program evaluation.

Instructional support for students can be enhanced with supplemental course software in the form of additional readings, practice exercises, homework, demonstrations, simulations, and sample tests. Other technology options might include web boards, listservs, class forums, remote access to tutors or the instructor via pagers, telephone, video, or the web, and additional and related web sites.

Presentation programs for giving demonstrations, showing charts, and explaining concepts have improved dramatically. Learning style inventories can be taken and scored on computers during a presentation. Any kind of workshop or presentation can include new and current information via the web and instant communication is possible with any telephone or internet accessible resource available anywhere in the world. Tutor training sessions or related activities can be available to tutors 24 hours/day, 7 days/week and can incorporate lectures, video segments, text documents, web sites, activities, chat rooms or other electronic forums, and assignments.

Communication options have exploded and now it is very easy via the web for students to find out about tutoring options without having to find the physical location or phone number. Providing information about study skill workshops, tutoring options, support for classes, advisement and testing options, or any other service provided is easy and inexpensive compared to past marketing strategies.

What about students with special needs?

Thanks for asking. The LSC or Learning Support Center on my campus is not the area that is responsible for providing accommodations for students with special needs, however, the LSC works with Special Services to support students' needs. Technology has provided these students with appropriate options to give them equitable access and support for learning. Some examples include listening enhancement devices, larger screen monitors or hardware or software which magnifies text, speech generating programs to provide audio feedback of on-screen or scanned text, voice recognition programs, spell checkers and language masters, and keyboard options for those who can not use both hands to type. Improved screen controls for fonts, colors, and size provide students with better options.

I am not sure I caught all the options you have mentioned, but it sounds great. What are some of the drawbacks with using technology?

The biggest drawback is the cost factor. Technology can quickly become the largest initial cost for beginning or expanding programs. Other key considerations include program needs, training in new technology, benefits and impact on program, access, space, maintenance of technology, and upgrades to replace obsolete technology. Too often LACs purchase software and equipment simply because it is new and innovative and the sales rep promised a panacea.

Without proper planning and strategies for implementation, new technology can become a two-edged sword. It may be cutting edge technology, but who is getting cut. New technology may have glitches that won't show up initially. Some of the new computer hardware and software companies release new products before exhaustive testing and bug clean-up. As problems occur, additional hardware or software "patches" are released to solve the problem—they may solve one problem and create another. Another major problem is that often users are not included in decisions regarding purchases of new technology or may not be aware of options available.

New technology can also require time from campus technical staff to be trained in new options, and time to set-up, test, and maintain new technology. Many users do not have a sense of time and staffing implications of adding new technology to an existing network or infrastructure in adding a new network.

Interesting, I had no idea that purchasing and using technology could be so complex. What are some things I could do to stay out of the technology traps you have described?

I would start with a needs assessment for technology. Get a group together to identify what is it you want to do. Check with other center directors to see what they do. Ask your technology savvy campus people for ideas. Gather information at conferences, via web sites or listservs, and from vendors. Be sure to have information on existing equipment and networks or have quick access to someone from your campus who knows. Before buying you may be able to have the sales folks visit your site and even provide a demonstration on your equipment or network. I have heard many horror stories of expensive technology that does not perform to expectations or needs and thus is not used.

The real key to the successful use of technology is in the planning. This includes: strategies for implementing, maintaining, and upgrading hardware and software; training all in the use of the new technology; and providing the support needed for users of the new technology. If the planning is done well, technology can be seen as an invaluable tool for program and service enhancement and effective use of limited resources.

Additional References

Brown, S., Carnahan, W., Kerstiens, G., & Maddaford, H. (1977). Technology with humanism supports learning. *Community and Junior College Journal*, 6-8, 27.

Caverly, D. (1995). Technology and the learning assistance center. In S. Mioduski & G. Enright (Eds.). *Proceedings of the 15th and 16th annual institutes for learning assistance professionals*, 1-14.

Caverly, D. (1995). Technology in learning centers: Past, present, future. In S. Mioduski & G. Enright (Eds.). *Proceedings of the 15th and 16th annual institutes for learning assistance professionals*, 15-34.

Christ, A. A. (1977). Videotaping: A useful technique for learning assistance practitioners. In G. Enright (Ed.), *Personalizing learning systems: Ecologies and strategies*. Proceedings of the tenth annual conference of the Western College Reading Association, 10, 115-118.

Christ, F. L. (1979). An audio tour of a university learning assistance center. *Technological Horizons in Education, 6, 1,* 50-51.

Christ, F. L. (1982). Computers in learning assistance centers and developmental education: Beginning to explore. *Journal of Developmental & Remedial Education*, 10-13.

Odom, M. L. (1992). *Incorporating new technologies into an academic assistance center*. Paper presented at fifth annual Midwest Regional Reading and Study Skills Conference, Kansas City, MO.

Rick Sheets was born in Indiana and has lived in Phoenix, AZ since 1960. In 1971, he became an Eagle Scout. He has worked in the Maricopa Community Colleges since 1982; worked in Learning Assistance from 1982-1998; has taught mathematics, reading, study skills, BASIC computer programming, Computer Applications, and Web Page Design, and is currently the Director of the Microcomputer Commons Lab at Paradise Valley Community College (about 500 computers including an Open lab and 11 computer classrooms). Rick earned a certificate as a Developmental Education Specialist from Appalachian State University (Kellogg Institute, 1985), became 4MAT ATS certified in Learning Styles (Excel, 1987) and completed his Ed.D. in Curriculum & Instruction at Arizona State University in 1994 (Dissertation: "The Effects of Training and Experience on Adult Peer Tutors in Community Colleges,"ASU, 1994). Rick has been awarded the League of Innovation's PVCC Innovator of the Year award twice. First, with Sally Rings in the development of a comprehensive tutor training program (which is CRLA ITCP certified) and second, as a team leader in the development of formal technology training options for campus staff and faculty. He has co-authored with Sally Krueger Rings two articles in the "Journal of Developmental Education" (content-related study skills and theoretical foundations for tutor training). Along with Frank Christ and Sylvia Mioduski, he also co-directs the annual Winter Institute and is the webster of the new Learning Support Center in Higher Education website. Rick is team-oriented, enjoys games, and is an active reader, computer addict, camper, music lover, and poet. His wife, partner, and friend is Barbara. His personal mission statement includes ". . . I want to continue to learn, grow, enjoy, and create; to integrate a part of me into all that I do . . ."

Question #10:
How Do I Assess What Programs and Services are Needed for Our Students?

A conversation with Gene Kerstiens

First of all, needs assessment is not so much a matter of selecting what programs and services are needed but rather where they will be offered, who will administer them, and how much effort should be afforded to budget, space, personnel, and equipment. Let me explain with an example. Tutoring will certainly be incorporated as one component of your program because its availability is a normal expectation on virtually all campuses. But the kind and amount of tutoring that is offered is the question that needs to be answered. And to assess this need and others, you should consult those most directly involved in student learning; for instance, students, faculty, counselors, and, of course, administrative officers and their selected staffs.

Are you suggesting that assessment will have political and organizational implications?

You bet! Although some players will want more voice than others, all must have their fingerprints appearing somewhere on the decision-making. Not every constituent may want to attend the party, but everyone will expect an invitation.

Then let's start with students. How might we get their input?

For starters, you might post a solicitation in the school newspaper to get random opinions. A more expedient and comprehensive method would be to administer paper-and-pencil surveys to a broad sample of students functioning at all levels of performance. Include those who had dropped classes and/or have departed from the institution. Commercially prepared instruments like the *College Student Needs Assessment Survey* could be employed. But this method is not preferred. Much more revealing, authentic, and detailed results yield from personally interviewing this same population. This is accomplished on a one-to-one basis or, more efficiently, in focus groups where the group dynamic elicits more spontaneous, spirited responses and prompts open discussion of learning problems students encounter in certain disciplines or classes.

That seems straightforward enough. But I'm more concerned about faculty input. Should I start by surveying the faculty senate?

You might want to advise and consult the faculty senate about your plans, especially if this body will endorse your efforts. But the interviews themselves might be more profitably conducted through academic departments or divisions. Consult first of all with deans or department heads to test the disciplinary climate. They may choose to name interested survey candidates among their faculty who could be interviewed personally. Also, you might ask to have some time during a division or department faculty meeting to discuss specific student learning problems of people who attend their classes. Incidentally, during these encounters you have an opportunity to identify faculty members whose enthusiasm would suggest their willingness to serve later on an advisory committee for the LAC when the center becomes operational. But don't be surprised if some disciplines show little interest in this process. You will, however, most likely encounter active interest among English, math, and science faculty.

Now, what about counselors? Should I use the same strategies on them?

Again, the dean of counseling services might be your best first contact to discuss strategy. But you will probably find that counselors prefer to interact one-on-one since they typically function in a more intimate, confidential setting. And the prompts used to elicit their responses could be adjusted to their style of operation. Doubtless, this group will have a different perspective on student needs involving emotional rather than intellectual obstacles to learning. Since they are not grade-givers and therefore not directly associated with instructional outcomes, what they hear from students will be different from and complementary to the picture that needs assessment is painting.

OK, speaking of the big picture, how will administrative personnel be put to use to fill out the assessment picture, which, apparently, is assuming the dimensions of a mural?

That's an incisive question—and observation! First of all, these information-driven players will be eager to learn the results of your assessment. Therefore, they will be most helpful as you gather data. Especially if a president, vice president, or academic dean refers you to a certain agency, the doors of that office will open more willingly to help you. For instance, your director of institutional research will have valuable enrollment, dropout, grade, testing, and other data and analyses, sometimes not otherwise shared or noticed. To investigate prudent hardware, software, and networking applications, the advice from the person in charge of campus technical systems can be priceless. The director of buildings and grounds can point out limitations and opportunities concerning space and location for the center. Identifying these and other needs can contribute to the assessment process.

Does that complete final touches to the needs assessment picture?

Hardly! Assessing needs is comparatively simple. Prioritizing programs and services included in your offerings will be more arduous. And as you develop and maintain the learning assistance center, hard choices are inevitable. Here is where you will encounter the realities of academic turf, disciplinary rivalries, budget, space allocations, and the shifting faculty and student sentiments toward instructional delivery. You may be the "new kid" on the academic block, so you'll be seeking accommodation from those well ensconced and sometimes recognized as sacred. Your negotiating talents will be tested. Good luck!

ADDITIONAL READINGS

Castelli, C., & De Johnson. (1984). Learning center assessment: Managing for change in the 80's. In D. R. Fleming (Ed.), *Journal of College Reading and Leaning*, 17, 30-42.

Clowes, D. (1981). Evaluation methodologies for learning assistance programs. In C. Walkever (Ed.), *Assessment of learning assistance services. New directions for college learning assistance.* San Francisco: Jossey-Bass, 17-32.

Miller, C., Dean, J. F., & McKinley, D. L. (1990). Learning approaches and motives: Male and female differences and implications for learning assistance programs. *The Journal of College Student Development*, 31, 147-154.

Gene Kerstiens, Founding Member of WCRA/CRLA, November 19, 1966 —President 1971—Editor, WCRA Proceedings, 1972-1975, Volumes 5-7— Archivist 1975-1977—Six Publications in the "WCRA Proceedings" & "Journal of College Reading and Learning."

Question #11:
What Kinds of Programs and Services Do LAC's Offer?

A conversation with Martha Maxwell

Comprehensive college learning assistance centers provide a variety of academic support services to students, faculty and staff. Larger institutions may have separate departments for each of these programs while smaller colleges may include most or even all of them under a learning assistance center umbrella. In establishing a learning center, concentrate on a few key programs first, based on a campus needs assessment and expand to other programs as circumstances permit. To be most effective, LAC directors must coordinate their programs and work closely with academic departments and other campus services.

Can you be more specific about learning assistance center programs?

Yes. Based on a review of the literature, here are some programs and services that many learning assistance centers offer.

◊ Testing services: the LAC may administer diagnostic and placement tests for individual students, assist faculty by administering course exams for LD or other disabled students who require special testing conditions, administer standardized tests, and proctor course make-up tests. At some small colleges, the LAC may even perform broader testing functions.

◊ Learning improvement programs: the LAC may diagnose student learning difficulties and prescribe appropriate activities, offer study skills workshops and learning strategies courses, distribute study skills information, partner with orientation programs, and train resident assistants to assist dorm students with their learning problems and concerns.

◊ Tutoring: the LAC sees tutoring as one of its more important components and may offer drop-in or scheduled tutoring individually and in small groups, on-line tutoring, tutor training, and tutor certification through programs like the CRLA Tutor Certification program.

◊ Supplemental Instruction: the LAC may administer an SI program in which it works with faculty of high risk courses to select, train, and supervise students who meet with groups of students from these courses to demonstrate and model successful learning strategies.

◊ Computer labs: the LAC may administer computer labs for instruction in basic skills like reading, writing, math, study skills, and critical thinking.

◊ Developmental course offerings: the LAC may offer credit and non-credit courses in reading, writing, math, study strategies, and critical thinking.

◊ Faculty services: the LAC may provide outreach services to faculty by demonstrating successful study strategies specific to their courses, describing its programs and services in selected classes, collaborating with faculty on teaching and learning research projects, and serving as a repository for course support materials.

◊ Referral service: the LAC may refer students to other campus departments such as counseling, campus ministry, health services, disabled student services, financial aid, academic advising, and career services.

That seems like a large list of programs and services that the LAC can offer. How do I decide what my LAC should offer?

If you are starting a learning assistance center, it is vital that you determine what functions are already being offered on your campus and who offers them. For example, you may want to set up a tutoring program and work toward gaining accreditation from CRLA, but find that there is a well-established writing center in the English department. Or you may want to offer help for those who suffer from test anxiety or math anxiety, a service already being offered by the counseling center or health service. Rather than duplicate services, work with other services through referrals and cooperative use of personnel, space, and materials.

Remember that specific functions will vary with each institution and the mission of the learning assistance center. In determining what services your center should offer, you need to know what existing services are available on your campus and figure how best they can be integrated with your learning services.

ADDITIONAL READINGS

Burns, M. E. (1986). Management strategies to assist students in improving learning skills. *Journal of Developmental Education*, (9) 3, 2-4.

Godsey, E. (1992). *The functions of a learning center.* Unpublished doctoral dissertation, Southern Missouri University.

Martin, D. C. (1980). Learning centers in professional schools. In K. V. Lauridsen (Ed.), *Examining the scope of learning centers. New directions for college learning assistance.* San Francisco: Jossey-Bass, 69-79.

Maxwell, M. (1978). *Improving student learning skills.* San Francisco: Jossey-Bass.

Maxwell, M. (1997). *Improving student learning skills: A new edition.* Clearwater, FL: H&H Publishing Company.

Martha Maxwell founded reading and study skills programs at American University, the University of Maryland, and the Student Learning Center at the University of California Berkeley. Throughout her professional life, Martha has been involved in the College Reading and Learning Association, notably providing conference presentations and workshops. As appreciation for her service to the profession, CRLA recognized Martha with the Silver Anniversary Award in 1992 and the Long and Outstanding Service Award in 1997. Since retiring from Berkeley 20 years ago, she has been active in professional associations and institutes, consulted, and written books and papers. Seven of her books have been published, the latest being "Improving Student Learning Skills, A New Edition", (1997) H&H Publishing Company.

Question #12:
How Do I Choose and Use Appropriate Instructional Resources for Students?

A conversation with Frank Christ

Let me answer this question in two parts: how to choose appropriate instructional resources and then how to use them.

First, let's talk about choosing instructional resources for students. The key word here is "students." Remember that students have different learning styles and abilities and you need to consider having available different types of instructional and self-help material for them. Think print material as well as audiocassettes, videos, and computer software. And think different reading levels of materials.

You can start choosing material by identifying your program needs. Then you can look for materials through Internet searches, the listserv LRNASST, CRLA and NADE national and regional conferences, reading of periodicals like *T.H.E. Journal*, *Journal of Developmental Education*, CRLA and NADE newsletters. You also can meet with faculty in key courses like Reading, English Comp, Ed Psych, Freshmen Orientation, Math, Study Skills, and ESL to get their recommendations for material that they think might benefit their students. By the way, consider keeping a "wish list" of materials that you want. You might even consider writing and filing for future use purchase orders for the materials that you would like to have available in the LAC.

I have a question. Since instructional resources today, especially multimedia materials, can be expensive, how can I know that what I am getting is useful?

Good question. It is one that many LAC directors don't get answers to before they actually purchase the material. Then they find out that it was not really useful for their students nor acceptable to faculty. Here is one solution. Before you purchase, send for a preview copy. Have one of your staff or an appropriate faculty member review it. Have one or more students sample it. On the basis of their feedback, make your decision to purchase or return it.

*That makes sense to me. Now, what about using these
materials that I have so carefully selected for use in the LAC?*

Before I answer that question, let me make a few suggestions on how the LAC can amass an enormous collection of materials and increase its reputation on campus as a resource for instructional and self-help materials without paying for many items.

You know that students will come or be referred to your LAC for assistance in study skills, writing and reading improvement, problem solving in math, physics, and chemistry, and, if your campus has many foreign students, English as a Second Language. Remember that on your campus many instructional and self-help materials already exist in the library, learning resource center, faculty offices, and campus bookstore. Your LAC could become the campus information resource for these materials by compiling a catalog of all available material.

*What you are recommending makes sense, but I am not clear
as to how I can do this.*

Okay. Let me step you through this. First, list all of the programs on campus that might have a collection of materials that would be useful for students. I have already suggested the campus library, learning resource center, faculty offices, and the campus bookstore. Visit these places and elicit their acceptance. Now comes the time-consuming part. Using database software like dBase, Access, or Fox Pro, start compiling this LAC master list. You may want to consider these fields for your database: physical location, instructional area, title, author, year of publication, type of media, and course applicability. When you have this list compiled, publicize to the campus that your LAC has it available. Keep a copy of this master list accessible to LAC staff, tutors, visiting faculty, and, of course, for students who will be asking for help. Oh, and by the way, you might consider asking faculty to donate materials for use in the center. If they do, design a bookplate that gives them credit for the donation and publicize their generosity in the campus newspaper or faculty newsletter.

*You mentioned the campus bookstore. Why include it in the
LAC master list of materials?*

The campus bookstore can be a great partner with the LAC if you work with it to have available for purchase a collection of study skills and self-help tutorial materials that you request. Some campus bookstores have a special section that displays material recommended by the LAC for student use. In addition, the bookstore can help publicize LAC programs and services by inserting your bookmarks in selected course texts or putting one or two of them in with purchases at the sales counter.

Please go back to my question that you have not yet answered. What about using these materials that I have so carefully selected?

When students come to the center for help and you feel that they can be helped with some program material, you might consider the following suggestions:

1. Give students a choice of available materials: text, audiovisual, computer-assisted.
2. Overview and model the material with students, especially if the material is software.
3. Let students know that a staff member is available if they have any problems with content or procedure as they use the material.
4. Get students to return when they have finished using the material. This is especially important when the student is going through material that has many chapters, modules, or sections. You may want to schedule appointments after each chapter or program module.
5. One last recommendation, have students evaluate the materials that they use. A simple form in which they grade the material from A to F and which has a place for their comments will tell you how successful you have been in supplying useful instructional and self-help material to students who come to your LAC.

ADDITIONAL READINGS

Flippo, R. F., & Caverly, D. C. (2000). *Handbook of college reading and study strategy research.* Mahway, NJ: Lawrence Erlbaum Publishers.

> *Frank L. Christ has been with CRLA all of its existence, beginning as a founding member in 1966 when he was at Loyola University, Los Angeles. Frank is a Past President (1968-69), editor of two WCRLA Proceedings (Combined Proceedings of the First, Second, and Third Annual Conferences and Proceedings of the Fourth Annual Conference, Newsletter Editorial Advisory Committee (1968-71), author of six articles, six of which were published in the association proceedings, recipient of Distinguished Leadership Award (1970), Distinguished Service Award (1972), and the Long and Outstanding Service Award (1986). Frank coined the phrases; "Learning Assistance Support System," "Learning Assistance Center," and "Learning Assistance" in a 1971 CRLA article. Frank was the director of the Learning Assistance Support System at CSU–Long Beach from 1972-1989 and is presently a Visiting Scholar with the University Learning Center–University of Arizona, where he co-directs the annual Winter Institute for Learning Assistance Directors and Practitioners. His email address is flchris@primenet.com.*

QUESTION #13:
HOW DO I ASSESS THE NEEDS OF INDIVIDUAL STUDENTS?

A conversation with Reed Mencke

I suggest we start by sketching the kinds of individual needs students are likely to bring to a Learning Assistance Center (LAC) for which assessment may be helpful. Obviously, the concerns students bring will be closely tied to the mission of your LAC and how that plays out in terms of specific roles. Three assessment roles are: 1) study skills, particularly text reading, notetaking, time management and test taking; 2) learning style assessment and 3) assessment of skills needed to master specific course content, particularly tutoring assessments, placement assessments, and basic skill assessments. Different kinds of assessment approaches are required for each area. And within areas we have a choice between "formal" and "informal" methods of assessment.

How do you distinguish between "informal" and "formal" assessment?

Informal assessment refers to any kind of non-standardized assessment. Formats for informal assessments include: direct observation of study behavior, interview questions, and the short quiz you make up on the spot to see where a student stands on some particular area such as time management. The possibilities are endless. At the University of Arizona we start every workshop with a short, informal assessment, typically a 5 to 10 item, "self-assessment" quiz, designed to ask workshop participants to think about the topic of the workshop.

Formal assessments are standardized instruments and are usually more carefully developed and structured than informal assessments. This development may include setting the assessment up in such a way that it can be taken and scored on a computer. An example of a formal assessment device would be a test like the MSLQ, Motivated Strategies for Learning Questionnaire, that has been normed to facilitate comparison of one student's result to a reference group such as "freshmen in science classes."

An informal assessment based on direct observation of behavior is often more useful than a formal assessment. For example, when discussing text reading I like to examine the student's text to see how they approach the task of text marking. If I'm helping a student with notetaking I assess a copy of the notes from the class they particularly want help with.

And in workshops I get the students to take responsibility for assessing their own work. I may, for example, ask them to look at and evaluate each other's style of notetaking using some guidelines such as Norm Stahl's criteria for good notes. Informal assessment combined with constructive feedback is the essential backbone of any intervention.

Can you describe some informal and formal methods of assessment? Would you start with study skills? I'm already finding that students don't always know what skills they need help with because they lack a clear model of what good study skills are.

Very true. And that means your first challenge may be to motivate them to consider doing an assessment of their study skills. You increase motivation by beginning with an informal assessment. First, ask your students to identify the one course they find most challenging this semester. Then ask to see a work sample from that course. The kind of sample depends on the content area. I always try to start by focusing our mutual attention on an area that is central to improved performance in their most challenging class. Students are practical. They expect us to be. Informal assessments, carefully tailored to the problem the student brings, serve to establish rapport and motivate. The students get immediate feedback on a task with which they have been struggling.

So far we have spoken only about informal assessments. Aren't there some formal devices, like paper and pencil tests and computer scored tests that we can use to help students assess study needs? I hear a lot about a test called LASSI.

There are a number of good formal assessment devices we use at the university and *LASSI, the Learning and Study Strategies Inventory*, is one of them. Others I consider useful are the *Survey of Reading/Study Efficiency II*, the *Student Behavior Inventory*, the *Motivated Strategies for Learning Questionnaire*, and the *Myers-Briggs Type Indicator*. It is handy to have one or more of these instruments available in your center and set up in such a manner that you can walk your student out for immediate on-the-spot assessment during the first conference.

I can see that the informal assessments you talked about earlier have the advantage of being inexpensive and relevant to the students. What do formal assessments offer?

One potential advantage of a formal assessment device is breadth of coverage. These instruments ask students a lot of questions, more than you have time to ask during a student interview. Potentially, you and the student get to look at the whole spectrum of study behavior. This may pinpoint problem areas that didn't come up in the interview. Equally important, you learn something about the student's strengths not just weaknesses. That allows for positive feedback, something we know is vital to self-esteem and making changes.

But each of the particular instruments has it's own particular set of strengths. Some are better for individual diagnosis, some for research, some allow you to insert customized recommendations that refer a student to LAC programs. The *SRSE II* was designed for individual and group sessions. The *SRSE II* and *SBI* have been set up so that your LAC can enter a set of customized recommendations that direct the student to particular LAC resource materials and programs or to other campus resources you want them to know about. *LASSI* is widely known, fairly inexpensive, and has been researched fairly extensively.

I have a question about student learning styles assessments. Are they useful?

Learning style inventories help faculty and tutors become more sensitive to individual differences in the learners they serve. I consider that to be their major utility. So we have built the *Myers-Briggs* and various other learning style assessments into our tutor-training program. And I sometimes use learning style assessments in student conferences. Taking a learning style inventory helps some students to understand themselves better. It can lead to a clearer picture of how they need to stretch their personal learning style to meet the teaching style of a particular instructor.

Can you sum up what you have said about the uses of assessment in the Learning Assistance Center?

Assessment is the essential ingredient of any effective academic intervention. Students lack information about where they stand in relation to effective study strategies, their personal learning style, and whether they have really attained mastery of key concepts in the courses they are taking. So any effort designed to help students improve should incorporate some good assessments that students understand and relate to. Often, in my experience, the simpler assessments work the best. But, for students motivated enough to take the time, formal assessments provide more thorough, comprehensive feedback. And certainly for situations where we are making decisions, we want a well-developed test that predicts success, in other words, a formal assessment.

What about the use of technology for assessment?

Technology can help us. It is helping us by making assessment available on the web, by providing interactive tutoring software that helps students process information more intensively and by providing forms of computer adaptive testing that make the placement process more friendly and accurate for our incoming students.

Technology is a tool the LAC can use, but we should use it always in a setting that is human and which provides the individual support that is a necessary condition for change in human behavior.

ADDITIONAL READINGS

Biggs, J. B. (1993). What do inventories of students' learning processes really measure? A theoretical review and a clarification. *British Journal of Educational Psychology*, (63), 3-19.

Bliss, L., & Mueller, R. (1994). *SBI (Study Behaviors Inventory)*. Rancho Palos Verdes, CA: Andragogy Associates.

Briggs, K., & Briggs Myers, I. (1990). *MBTI (Myers-Briggs Type Indicator)*. Palo Alto, CA: Consulting Psychologists Press, Inc.

Christ, F. L. (1985). *SRSE II (Survey of Reading/Study Efficiency)*. Sierra Vista, AZ: Personal Efficiency Programs.

Pintrich, P., Smith, D., Garcia, T., & McKeachie, W. (1991). *MSLQ (Motivated Strategies for Learning Questionnaire)*. Ann Arbor, MI: University of Michigan.

Weinstein, C., Schulte, A., & Palmer, D. (1987). *LASSI (Learning & Study Strategies Inventory)*. Clearwater, FL: H&H Publishing Company.

Reed Mencke joined the University Learning Center of the University of Arizona as Associate Director July, 1993. Prior to that he held positions at the U of A as Associate Director of Counseling, Lecturer in Psychology, and Associate Director and Director of Student Affairs Research. Reed's publications span the fields of psychology instruction, psychological counseling, institutional research and college student learning and development. Most recently he initiated a partnership between the University Learning Center and a group of general education faculty called Teaching Teams. This project has received three year funding from the Fund for Improvement of Post Secondary Education (FIPSE) and the Kellogg Foundation and has been described as "highly transformational" by an independent evaluation team from UCLA's ACE program. Reed served as a mentor at the Winter Institute, January, 1999. At U of A he has designed and conducted tutor training programs for a credit tutor training class (MCB 497a) in the Department of Molecular and Cellular Biology as well as for the Preceptor Program. He works closely with the Department of Geosciences and, with Peter Kresan has designed a series of study strategy workshops that are integrated into the introductory geology course. Mencke, Kresan and others co-authored a new instructor manual for introductory geology courses that incorporates learning principles into the teaching of geology.

QUESTION #14:
HOW ARE LEARNING ASSISTANCE CENTERS STAFFED AND MANAGED?

A conversation with Rick Sheets

The staffing and management of a center depends upon many considerations. The typical role of the LAC administrator is to provide leadership and vision for the center. Ideally, the center administrator can also become a catalyst or change agent for the institution. Often the reality is that the administrator is placed in a position with many responsibilities and programs and too little staffing and inadequate funding. Many of the new managers of centers have little management experience and often do not know how to delegate tasks. This reality often finds center administrators operating in a crisis management mode which can lead to burnout and stress related problems. Having the right learning assistance center staff can be a critical key for the success of the program.

What are some program management tools for an administrator wishing to avoid a management-by-crisis mode?

A process to systematically assess needs, establish goals, build teams, monitor progress, and evaluate effectiveness should be used. Three proven, effective, and comprehensive models include Management by Objective, MBO; Total Quality Management, TQM; and Continuous Quality Improvement, CQI. Three newer models focusing on team-building and leadership include "Gung Ho Teams" by Ken Blanchard, "WOW Projects" by Tom Peters, and "Seven Habits of Highly Effective People" by Stephen Covey.

New models are emerging all the time. Peters' past focus of a "Search for Excellence" has moved to his new model of "WOW Projects." Blanchard's past focus of a "One Minute Manager" now has moved to that of creating and maintaining a "Hi-Performance Team." If a management model is being initiated at your institution, a pilot that incorporates this method may have a better chance for support and funding. Any model that promotes excellence, quality, team building, and customer service can validate what is being done well and can be incorporated into a program. Any of these models can help managers to share the "load" of the center with their staff and enjoy the process of managing.

Is it important to keep records?

A good question. Thanks for asking. Programs with accurate statistics which document services, level of use, and successes have a stronger chance of receiving funds and support for continued existence or expansion. A well-documented history of service, use, and success can often stave off or minimize the inevitable budget cuts. I would suggest you:

1. give an annual report of the number of students served by the center and their demographics;
2. report any success outcomes, survey results and student evaluations;
3. report faculty and/or student perceptions of the center's programs;
4. identify anything else which will illustrate the success of the program such as student or faculty evaluations; and
5. keep statistics to show growth and long term trends.

So the three words to remember are document, Document, DOCUMENT!

How are most centers funded?

Initial funding for a learning assistance program is very often unique to the institution. Often initial funding is a pilot within a department or an institution. Frequently, a short-term internal or external grant is available to pilot a new program. It is important to establish a network for program support at all levels possible and to establish continuing funding sources to continue beyond the pilot stage.

Even when successful, programs have been abandoned when budget monies are tight. Statistics documenting successes, a cost-versus-benefit analysis, combined with stated support from the faculty, administration, program heads, and students can help new centers get established, survive institutional budget cuts, and even expand.

You have mentioned funding concerns several times. Do you have any suggestions for keeping operating costs down initially?

Yes, there are several things you may want to consider. The major cost in the past has been staffing. Providing current textbooks for tutor use has also been another major cost. Providing current technology such as microcomputers has recently become another major program cost. In addition to working to cut costs, you may also want to look at ways to generate income.

For staffing costs, look at hiring students where feasible. Many successful programs employ mainly students as their tutors and initial clerical staff. Check into cost-saving student options like college workstudy, graduate assistants, service learning projects, co-op projects, credit courses for education majors, internships, and independent projects. Identify and market a volunteerism component to your program for retirees, especially teachers or engineers, service organizations like YMCA, and campus clubs such as honors clubs. Faculty can also be a great and cost-effective resource if they use part of their required office hours or committee work in the learning assistance center tutoring, working with tutors, and/or developing materials to support their students.

To provide current textbooks as a resource for tutors you can: 1) hire students who have taken the class recently and have a copy; 2) ask instructors who may have received a preview copy in addition to a desk copy and may be willing to loan it or give it to a center; 3) solicit a free desk or preview copy from your bookstore or the publisher by contacting them and letting them know your need; or 4) ask for textbook donations from students as they complete a class.

For computers or other technology, check with local vendors and suggest they loan you a computer with the company logo and contact information. Your institution may also have some partnership programs or grants which include providing computers. Ask to be included in funding considerations in new programs or partnerships so that your center can support their efforts as well.

What are some key strategies I could employ initially to build a strong staff?

After identifying the rationale, the mission of the learning assistance center, and the staffing needs of the program, it may be appropriate to discuss and develop an organizational chart of the staffing of the center. Many centers are funded from student services, academic services, grant or other soft money, or within a specific department's budget. Reporting structure and budgets are not required to follow the same lines, though often they do. Generally speaking, the major source of funding identifies the reporting structure. Once staffing is in place, begin establishing good communication, a common purpose, roles, and expectations with all staff. If you have options as to the reporting structure of the program, consider the best place for support and funding.

The center administrator should be reporting to a dean, president, or provost if possible. It is usually best to not have the center ultimately housed under a department or program if it is to serve students for the whole institution.

What kinds of qualifications should staff have?

Qualifications can be considered once the type of staff positions needed are determined and may differ depending on the expectations and responsibilities of the staffing positions selected and the amount of training provided. General qualification considerations include content expertise, which can be documented through degrees earned, coursework, grades, and work experience.

In the area of content expertise needed for positions in faculty and management, background should include degrees and should reflect experience at a credible level. Qualifications should include:
◊ prior experience in working with college students;
◊ knowledge of the academic and emotional skills needs of the student population to be served;
◊ ability to listen and communicate effectively with diverse student populations and other staff in the center and in the institution and to deal with the students' affective and academic problems with patience and understanding and yet know when to be firm;
◊ understanding of the institution's policies and procedures;
◊ good group and one-to-one communication skills;
◊ analytical and problem-solving skills;
◊ flexibility in adapting skills development techniques to students' needs rather than forcing students into predetermined skills approach;
◊ open to learning about the skills development programs of other professionals in the center and other colleagues in the field and willing to integrate new information and programs and tailor them to the needs of students using the center; and
◊ commitment to the center with quality service to students.

Since a large portion of my staff will be tutors, do you have suggestions for recruitment?

It is difficult to find, recruit, and keep tutors because of the nature of the center. Many students feel overcommitted and unable to add another responsibility to their load. As they complete their program, they are usually gone. Retirees generally offer longer and more sustained service as tutors, but there are some ways to recruit and retain students too.

Benefits for students as tutors which can be offered and marketed to recruit tutors include: letting tutors set their own flexible schedule; tutoring provides reinforcement of concepts learned; tutoring "harder" courses looks good on resumes; and tutors' supervisors would be available as references for a future job application. Also offer a little higher wage than the average student wage on your campus. Incorporating an internationally recognized tutor training certification program can help to establish program credibility with students and faculty and encourage students to become tutors.

Instructors can become your greatest recruiters for tutors. Have them refer students they see as potential tutors to you. This provides "buy-in" for faculty, helps students to plan for the possibility of being tutors for the coming semester, builds credibility for your center, and gives you a pool of applicants as tutors. This works especially well for higher levels of sequenced courses or specialized program, or for a Supplemental Instruction program. Providing training for staff will enhance the consistency and quality of services provided. Certifying tutors as part of an internationally recognized program such as "International Tutor Certification Program" (ITCP) will greatly enhance the program's credibility with students, staff, and faculty.

In addition to tutors, what other staff might I need?

After deciding upon the program and services that will be included within the LAC, a next consideration should be to look at staff and options needed to support those programs. The staff may include faculty, managers, support staff, temporary workers, students, or volunteers.

Staff responsibilities may include teaching, coordinating programs or activities, supervising other staff or students, providing study skills workshops or seminars, advising, developing individualized learning packages or plans, tutoring, testing, proctoring, grading, evaluating programs, recordkeeping, reporting, giving tours, developing materials, demonstrating resources or software, promotion and public relations, monitoring budget or payroll, scheduling appointments, and may include clerical tasks such as word processing, typing, filing, checking out resources, and maintaining data bases and spreadsheets.

Initially more creative part-time staffing needs may be met by sharing staff with other departments; having faculty use LAC time as a committee assignment, as part of their required office hours, or as part of a teaching load; using internal or external grants to provide staff, or developing internships or credit-bearing experiences for students.

What other tips or suggestions do you have for managing an effective LAC?

Communication is probably the most critical key for managing an efficient and effective program. It can be a challenge to establish and maintain good communication because of the varied schedules and part-time nature of many of the tutors. A good start would be to establish regular staff meetings that can help to keep all staff abreast of changes and continuing expectations. Mailboxes or staff cubbies can provide a place for staff to regularly check in and receive information updates. Foster strong affiliations between full-time and part-time staff. Encourage special efforts to keep part-time staff informed. Electronic mail can be an easy and effective communication tool for center top-down, bottom-up, and peer discussions, announcements, and information updates. Ongoing anonymous written student evaluations of any staff, collected and returned frequently, can provide more honest communications to staff and supervisor as they provide insight into students' perceptions of staff performance. An open-door policy for any staff to talk with supervisors or center administrators can also keep communications flowing. Inviting faculty, institution administration, and/or students to center events such as pot luck, open houses, and tours, can help open many levels of communication and increase positive atmosphere in the center.

Keep your campus administrators informed regularly. Include campus administrators and governing board members in center events like the Tutor Certification Award Ceremony. Each communication offers an opportunity to educate those involved as to the purpose, needs, and successes of your program. An example is that a note to your campus president of an increase in students served is something he/she could use in communications about campus services. Keep the reports brief, inviting, and informative.

I strongly believe in individual contacts. They can build teams, enhance understanding, and improve communications. Thus, I see each contact as time well spent and a crucial component for managing the LAC program. Finally, take care of yourself—"Slow down to the speed of life." Many LAC professionals burn out because they care about others at the expense of themselves. Take care of yourself, do your best, and enjoy the process!

ADDITIONAL READINGS

Blanchard, K., & Bowles, S. (1997). *Gung ho!: Turn on the peolple in any organization.* New York: William Morrow & Company.

Caputo, E. (1989). Learning center model and administration. *Issues in College Learning Centers,* (9), 55-61.

Carlson, R., & Bailey, J. (1997). *Slowing down to the speed of life.* New York: Harper Collins.

Covey, S. (1990). *7 habits of highly effective people: Powerful lessons in personal change.* New York: Simon & Schuster.

Fujitaki, N. (1974). CSULB intern training in learning assistance. In G. Kerstiens (Ed.), *Reading update: Ideals to reality.* Seventh annual proceedings of the Western College Reading Association, 83-90.

Garcia, S. (1981). The training of learning assistance practitioners. In F. L. Christ & M. Coda-Messerle (Eds.). *Staff development for learning support systems. New directions for college learning assistance.* San Francisco: Jossey-Bass, 4, 29-37.

Maxwell, M. (1990). "Does Tutoring Help?" A Look at the Literature. *Review of Research in Developmental Education, 7,* (4), 1-5.

Peters, T. (1997). *The pursuit of WOW.* New York: Vintage Books.

Roueche, S. D. (1983). Elements of program success: Report of a national study. In J. E. Roueche (Ed.), *A new look at successful programs. New directions for college learning assistance.* San Francisco: Jossey-Bass, 3-10.

Sheets, R. A. (1994). *The effects of training and experience on adult peer tutors in community colleges.* Doctoral dissertation, Arizona State University, 1-5.

Smith, K., & Brown, S. (1981). Staff performance evaluation in learning assistance centers. In C. Walkever (Ed.), *Assessment of learning assistance services. New directions for college learning assistance.* San Francisco: Jossey-Bass, 95-110.

Rick Sheets was born in Indiana and has lived in Phoenix, AZ since 1960. In 1971, he became an Eagle Scout. He has worked in the Maricopa Community Colleges since 1982; worked in Learning Assistance from 1982-1998; has taught mathematics, reading, study skills, BASIC computer programming, Computer Applications, and Web Page Design, and is currently the Director of the Microcomputer Commons Lab at Paradise Valley Community College (about 500 computers including an Open lab and 11 computer classrooms). Rick earned a certificate as a Developmental Education Specialist from Appalachian State University (Kellogg Institute, 1985), became 4MAT ATS certified in Learning Styles (Excel, 1987) and completed his Ed.D. in Curriculum & Instruction at Arizona State University in 1994 (Dissertation: "The Effects of Training and Experience on Adult Peer Tutors in Community Colleges,"ASU, 1994). Rick has been awarded the League of Innovation's PVCC Innovator of the Year award twice. First, with Sally Rings in the development of a comprehensive tutor training program (which is CRLA ITCP certified) and second, as a team leader in the development of formal technology training options for campus staff and faculty. He has co-authored with Sally Krueger Rings two articles in the "Journal of Developmental Education" (content-related study skills and theoretical foundations for tutor training). Along with Frank Christ and Sylvia Mioduski, he also co-directs the annual Winter Institute and is the webster of the new Learning Support Center in Higher Education website. Rick is team-oriented, enjoys games, and is an active reader, computer addict, camper, music lover, and poet. His wife, partner, and friend is Barbara. His personal mission statement includes ". . . I want to continue to learn, grow, enjoy, and create; to integrate a part of me into all that I do . . ."

QUESTION #15:
HOW WILL THE LAC FIT INTO THE INSTITUTION'S ORGANIZATIONAL STRUCTURE?

A conversation with Gwyn Enright

That was the key question asked in California in the late 1970's when learning assistance centers were proliferating. Ideally, the LAC would enjoy an administrative alliance that would allow interdisciplinary offerings and technological support. Ideally, the LAC would also have the administrative ties necessary to offer credit for classes and training and to include faculty respected by other campus academicians on the LAC staff. In this fantasy, the LAC would also be situated administratively so it had its own funding and didn't have to compete with other departments yearly or have to plan from grant to grant.

So, you've described your fantasy. What was the reality?

Of course, the actuality of where the LAC lies in the organizational structure has much to do with the history of the institution and the existing political realities. Using California as an example, at California State University Northridge, the Learning Resource Center had two lines of reporting! The director reported to the dean of student services and the site reported to the dean of the university, who was essentially the vice president of academic affairs. In addition, the LRC was responsible to the head of library services for the facility. At San Diego City College, the Independent Learning Center director reported to the head librarian. At California's El Camino College, the LAC reported to the dean of instruction. The LAC at California State University–Long Beach, once under student services moved to academic affairs.

You're talking solely about California. What does this mean for the other 49 states?

Sorry about that. Let me think in more general terms. The LAC can be placed under student services or counseling, thus usually insuring the involvement of learning skills counselors and professionals adept at addressing the affective domain. Also, the LAC then is not viewed as a competitor for academic departmental funding and is well placed to be a service agency for the whole campus. On the other hand, the LAC can be placed under academic affairs or instruction. Then the LAC often enjoys more credibility with the content area faculty and usually offers credit for classes and even for tutor or paraprofessional training. The LAC can be part of a separate University College which is an academic unit designed to enroll and support special populations, or the LAC can even be funded through student fees.

What is the most important organizational consideration?

Placing the LAC where it serves the largest cross section of the campus population. That's why I think one of the most important questions to ask in planning the LAC is, "Where can we serve the greatest population?" Even though there are so many models available, guidelines don't have to be complicated. In the middle of the flurry of opinions about where an LAC truly belongs administratively, a practitioner at a professional meeting asked Martha Maxwell about this. Martha replied, "Put it where the power is."

ADDITIONAL READINGS

Carpenter, K. (1985). A place for learning centers in the administrative structure of postsecondary institutions. *Forum for Reading, 17*, 1, 23-27.

Whyte, C. S. (1980). An integrated counseling and learning center. In K. V. Lauridsen (Ed.), *Examining the scope of learning centers. New directions for college learning assistance.* San Francisco: Jossey-Bass, 33-43.

Gwyn Enright served as CRLA President in 1987. She had been Editor of the Proceedings from 1978 to 1981 and has published articles on test support programs and on the national status and history of learning assistance in the WCRLA/CRLA Proceedings and the Journal of College Reading and Learning. She received the CRLA Long and Outstanding Service Award in 1996.

QUESTION #16: WHERE ARE LAC PROGRAMS AND SERVICES LOCATED?

A conversation with Gwyn Enright

Let me answer this facetiously. The learning assistance center has a near cult tradition of being located out of sight—far away in a temporary barracks on the edge of campus or buried in the deep bowels of a dank building. Ideally, the learning assistance center should be centrally located so learners can find it. It should be visible to decision-makers and potential clients, and so the campus as a whole owns the center and the services it provides.

A good place is the library or the learning resource center because they are usually centrally located and often have the environmental flexibility needed to offer learners technological alternatives to content mastery and learning skills improvement. As campuses start to implement plans for new buildings, it would be good for the LAC professionals to be involved in the planning.

What if a central location is not an option for the LAC?

While that means some loss of visibility and some duplication, smaller units in different departments can mean more convenience for students and more commitment from the faculty. An inspired publicity campaign can still guarantee visibility for the learning assistance center even when it is not centralized in one prime location.

Additional Readings

Lissner, L. S. (1989). College learning assistance programs: The results of a national survey. *Issues in College Learning Centers*, 9, 82-95.

Lissner, L. S. (1990). The learning center from 1829 to the year 2000 and beyond. In R. M. Hashway (Ed.), *Handbook of developmental education*. New York: Praeger Publishers, 127-154.

Smith, G. D., Enright, G., & Devirian, M. (1975). A national survey of learning and study skills programs. In G. H. McNich & W. D. Miller (Eds.). *Reading: Convention and inquiry*. Clemson, SC: National Reading Conference Proceedings, 67-73.

Gwyn Enright served as CRLA President in 1987. She had been Editor of the Proceedings from 1978 to 1981 and has published articles on test support programs and on the national status and history of learning assistance in the WCRLA/CRLA Proceedings and the Journal of College Reading and Learning. She received the CRLA Long and Outstanding Service Award in 1996.

Question #17:
What Are Some Space, Furnishings, and Equipment Considerations in the Design of the LAC?

A conversation with Karen Smith

The crucial factor upon which all your decisions will be made is the mission, or purpose, for your learning center. Why is this new LAC being put in place? To respond to faculty's wishes that all students have out-of-class support for their courses? To effect a change in the attrition rate and improve students' long term chances for success by initiating new mechanisms for study? To bolster the skills of marginal students who appear to be unsuccessful in your college's educational programs? To serve special populations who have been underserved and less successful than the majority? If the mission is focused to a special population or a special need, then the amount of space to be dedicated to the center will be limited as well. On the other hand, if the plan is to serve a large percent of the student body, then the space must be adequate to allow for a variety of activities and easy flow to and from the various services of the LAC.

How do I plan for the best use of my existing space?

Really, a first question to ask yourself is, will the students be required to come to the LAC for specific assistance? If so, remember that required participation will dictate space parameters because you can assume that use of services will be automatic and at peak the day the center is opened and not grow gradually over time.

In addition, consider the various services that will be offered within the facility. Adequate space to allow for classes, computer lab use, open tutoring, and other activities must be accounted for, especially if all activities will operate in unison. If you have classrooms and they are not used during the entire day for classes, then the space can be used for tutoring during other periods. However, if tutoring needs are extensive, then tutoring will operate all day and a dedicated area will be required exclusive of any available classrooms.

The reason for your LAC—its goals, its mission—will dictate the larger notion of space requirements.

Will I face different problems if I plan a learning assistance center for a designated space versus designing the shape of the space?

If you are given the option to design a new facility for your LAC, you can optimize all aspects of your program. What great fun to be able to do this! If, however, a designated space is to be remodeled for the LAC, you may find yourself facing difficult and surprising constraints. You can, with careful planning and prioritizing, provide for all aspects of the program that you have planned, even in a relatively small area.

In the learning assistance centers that I supervise, we provide the same basic services in each of the five centers. However, the spaces vary greatly from 8,000 to 1,400 square feet. Granted, within the largest facility, more computers are available and the tutoring area is much larger. In addition, this largest center has a comfortable conference room where workshops and staff meetings can be held. But even the smallest center has computers, learning assistance carrels, and an open tutoring area, as well as offices for the director and learning specialist, a dedicated area for the secretary and learning assistants, an office work area and reception desk.

Although the site allocated for your learning center may not fit your preferences, you can, with careful consideration and planning, place your planned activities in almost any space provided. One must determine what percentage of space will be dedicated to each service of the LAC, and then work within the space allocated. It can be done.

How do I go about determining the specific furnishings for the LAC?

Most likely, by the time that you have delineated the learning center's mission, thought through carefully and planned the use of the dedicated space, the identification of specific furnishings will follow easily. Think about not only functionality but also versatility in making a final decision on furniture. If furniture is purchased with only one purpose in mind and one place to use it, you lose the option of moving furnishings around as needs may change. On the other hand, some furnishings must be identified for specific purposes. Computer tables are definitely recommended for computers over something like library tables, which can accommodate tutoring but are awkward and improperly designed for computing use.

Actually, your college may not only provide you with the assistance of an interior designer or consultant but may also dictate the vendors from which you must purchase your furniture. State or college contracts with furniture vendors allow for a maximization of funds for the purchase of furniture, office equipment such as phones, fax machines, and often computers, printers, and copiers as well. If a consultant is available to you, be sure that you explain the goals and philosophy of your service carefully, because a consultant who has not been involved in designing for a program like a learning center will need close collaboration with you in making the right selections.

What other issues should concern me?

Obviously, an inviting atmosphere is crucial to an effective learning assistance center. The learning center should be very open and friendly. We want our students to be eager to use our services, and they are often initially shy about seeking assistance for something that they perceive others not needing. Lots of windows, if possible, and open working areas encourage even the most reticent student to see and be seen as one of many students "doing what comes naturally."

I personally have a strong negative attitude about any learning assistance center facility that uses a medical model. Such a facility provides a series of closed-door areas much too similar to the doctor's examining room where you learn about your affliction—or academic problem—and may be given a prescription for a remedy—guidance and assistance. If we want our students to feel secure and welcome in seeking learning assistance, then the facility must reflect that attitude and ambiance.

Another serious concern is accessibility for anyone needing special accommodations. In all likelihood, your college will have an individual who is responsible for monitoring for ADA and Section 504 compliance and can assist you in this area. However, you must be cognizant of how students with special needs will access the learning assistance center services and plan for their needs.

In identifying necessary equipment, do guidelines exist for making my decisions?

I must begin an answer to this question by referring you back to the mission or purpose for your learning assistance center, for from that you will determine the kinds of equipment that will be needed to provide the services of your center. Your college may provide very strict parameters for the vendors that you use for purchases, or it may provide only guidelines, and you must make the decisions. In addition, the CAS Standards for Learning

Assistance Programs contains a section on facilities and equipment among its 13 sections, and this may be beneficial to you as a guide.

I remember the confusion and bafflement that I experienced when first trying to determine which kinds of projectors, or tape players I should purchase for my new learning assistance center. The university was willing to offer catalogs for my use, but I found that I was really on my own in the final decision. So, I began to use the small network of colleagues in other learning centers and asked for their sage advice. On the whole, my decisions turned out to be wise and the equipment served us well and assisted the staff in delivering the services that we had promised in our mission.

How will I know now what will be needed in the future?

Well, you are now planning for the present and much of your plans will be based on a "good faith" use of space. In other words, you may have much documentation of academic needs and great ideas for providing services to accommodate and resolve these needs, but you can never be certain of the expediency of your plans until the students walk through the doors. And, likewise, you cannot know today exactly how the use of services may grow and expand.

But, and this is important, you were hired for the position and given the responsibility for making the decisions, so your good judgement is important. Again, call on your colleagues who have been in this field for some time and ask good questions about program growth and expansion. Did their centers experience a natural growth, slowly and incrementally over the years? Or was there a sudden discovery of the learning assistance center by the students in the second or third year, which brought about a surge of users? Did your colleagues experience program growth due to program expansion or an assignment of a new service to the learning assistance center?

In addition, study the student population in your college and use the information about their characteristics in making your decisions. Ask your dean or institutional research director for student information that can provide an indication—really only a clue—about how your students will access a new service, and how likely they are to respond to academic support.

So, are you saying that I should plan for a lot of growth in the use of my center's services?

Sure, don't you expect an increase in use each year? I'm really suggesting that if the space is adequate for meeting the initial needs of your planned activities, and there is space for which you cannot now conceive a use— keep it and develop a flexible-use plan. Remember the old adage, "Your possessions will grow to fill your cupboards and closets?" This is an excellent time to protect space and allow for its unexpected or not-yet-planned use.

But, above all, have fun in designing your center. This is your big opportunity to live out some of your dreams for a learning assistance center, and you will want to capitalize on as many as possible now.

ADDITIONAL READINGS

Hashway, R. M. (1989). Developmental learning center designs. *Research and Teaching in Developmental Education, (5)*, 2, 25-38.

Karwin, T. J. (1973). *Flying a learning center: Design and costs of an off-campus space for learning.* Berkeley, CA: Carnegie Commission on Higher Education.

White, W. G., Jr., & Schnuth, M. L. (1990). College learning assistance centers: Places for learning. In R. M. Hashway (Ed.), *Handbook of developmental education.* New York: Praeger, 155-177.

White, W. G., Jr., Kyzar, B., & Lane, K. E. (1990). College learning assistance centers: Spaces for learning. In R. M. Hashway (Ed.), *Handbook of developmental education.* New York: Praeger, 179-195.

White, W. G., Jr., Kyzar, B., & Lane, K. E. (1990). College learning assistance center design considerations. *The Educational Facility Planner, (28)*, 4, 22-26.

Karen G. Smith is currently the University Director of the Learning Resource Centers of Rutgers University. She has the distinction of designing, developing and directing learning assistance centers in three unique and different universities: Rutgers University, Tulane University, and New Mexico State University. Karen is a 25-year member of CRLA, is a past president (1983-84), NM state director (1975-77), workshop presenter at many conferences, and is currently archivist (1986-) and a member of the JCRL Editorial Board (1997-). One of her proudest achievements is recognition by her peers in CRLA with the Long and Outstanding Service Award. In addition to her commitment to her membership in CRLA, Karen is a long-standing member of IRA and served as the New Mexico State President in 1977. She has consulted widely with other colleges and universities for over 20 years, in learning assistance center design and development, reading education in colleges and universities, and management and supervision in learning centers.

Question #18:
How Can LAC Programs and Services Be Evaluated?

A conversation with David Gerkin

There are many ways to evaluate LAC programs and services, but before we begin to explore some of the methods, I think it is important to discuss the benefits of evaluation.

That sounds reasonable. What are some of the benefits?

Some benefits include justifying your program's existence and improving its chances of continuation and expansion, or at least maintenance, of financial, material, and human resources. Reports to your college administrators can be quite helpful in maintaining or increasing your resource allocation. Be sure to demonstrate effective use of resources, indicating increasing numbers of students utilizing your services, and showing the need for additional resources.

Another benefit of evaluation is program improvement: learning what works and what does not, what you are doing well, and what needs improvement. For example, you can gather data to help determine if your marketing efforts are bringing students into your programs, if tutors are having an impact on students' learning and growth, if students are satisfied with their interaction with particular tutors, and if your tutor training program is having an effect on how your tutors work with students.

In addition, what we learn from our evaluation can help us make better decisions about our programs and services, and, in fact, one of the reasons for undertaking evaluation is to help with decision making.

I know my college's administrators like to see reports with numbers, but I think some of my program's best data is anecdotal: students' comments about how our program has helped them to be successful students. Is this a useful way of evaluating our program?

Absolutely! When combined with reports indicating numbers of students using services, anecdotal data can bring the numbers to life and make the reports more meaningful and powerful.

This has all been quite interesting, but let's get back to my original question; how can I evaluate my programs and services?

If you are asking how you can gather the data, some possibilities include formal or informal instruments such as questionnaires calling for written responses in the form of open-ended questions and/or forced choice questions, surveys on Scantron forms, questionnaires using rating scales such as the Likert scale, computer programs that help you gather and organize data, brainstorming sessions, and reflective journaling.

That gives me some methods to use, but the question that occurs to me now is, "What data should I gather?"

Some of your choices are statistics of usage, which can include: the number of users of your services, number of contacts with your center, and demographic information on users of your services. Other data could include evaluation of tutors by users and supervisors, of program effectiveness by users and tutors, of tutor training by tutors, of program quality by staff, of staff by manager, and of manager by staff.

You have mentioned evaluation of various aspects of programs and services by users of services, tutors, staff, and managers. Are there others who should be asked to evaluate my program? What about faculty?

Yes, faculty evaluation of your programs and services can be very useful. Faculty input and feedback can help you build a program that supports what faculty are doing in the classroom and provides more relevant instructional support to students. In addition to strengthening your program, asking for faculty insights and constructive criticism can help you improve communication and collaboration with them that can be crucial to the success of your program.

I have found asking faculty for information regarding awareness and ratings of my programs and services helpful. I have also solicited input regarding which services they have recommended and/or would recommend to students.

Outside consultants may also be asked to evaluate your program. A colleague from another institution may be invited to visit your program and provide an evaluation with a fresh perspective. These evaluations can be arranged as a trade: you evaluate your colleague's program, and she, in turn, evaluates yours. An outside consultant can pose as a student and interact with your staff to get an honest sense of what a student's experience is like.

Evaluations from an outsider's view can give you very useful feedback that you would never get from someone close to your organization.

We've talked about the who, what, and how of evaluation, what we haven't covered is when.

Most programs are asked to produce an annual report, but I would suggest utilizing end of term and ongoing evaluations as well. Of course, some of the data from your end of term and ongoing evaluations will probably end up in your annual report, but I think it is beneficial to analyze and reflect on the data you are collecting on a regular basis.

A specific example of an ongoing evaluation used in our center is a three-part carbon form on which students evaluate tutors. This provides not only a rating of the tutor, but, often, excellent anecdotal data in the comment section that I used to supplement my statistical reports. The students are not asked to identify themselves on the form and are instructed to place the completed forms in a closed container in the hope that anonymity will provide us with more honest responses. These ongoing evaluations provide us with timely feedback on tutor performance to reinforce positive behavior and deal appropriately with any concerns or potential problems.

A final word on annual reports. Many administrators appreciate a short, concise annual report; for example, a one-page report with bullets highlighting major accomplishments and improvements. When presenting this to the president, dean, or other administrator, have the supporting details and complete reports available in case questions arise.

Now that I've gathered all this data, how do I compile it so I can analyze and reflect on it, report it, and use it to inform my decision making?

Depending on the hardware and software available to you, options include entering data into a database to organize it and create reports. You can use Scantron forms that feed data into a database and allow you to print reports with charts and graphs. Use word processing software to compile summaries of written responses, and use a spreadsheet to calculate percentages of user demographics and usage statistics. Your institutional researcher on your campus can be an invaluable resource in providing you with help in designing data gathering instruments, compiling and analyzing data, and formatting reports.

ADDITIONAL READINGS

Baker, G. A., & Painter, P. L. (1983). The Learning center: A study of effectiveness. In J. E. Roueche (Ed.), *A new look at successful programs. New directions for college learning assistance.* San Francisco: Jossey-Bass, 73-88.

Brown, R. R. (1980). Evaluating learning centers. In O.T. Lenning & R. Nayman (Eds.). *New roles for learning assistance. New directions for college learning assistance.* San Francisco: Jossey-Bass, 75-92.

Castelli, C., & De Johnson. (1984). Learning center assessment: Managing for change in the 80's. In D. R. Fleming (Ed.), *Journal of College Reading and Learning,* 17, 30-42.

Christ, F. L. (1978). Management is evaluation. *Audiovisual Instruction, (23),* 8, 26, 62.

Clowes, D. (1981). Evaluation methodologies for learning assistance programs. In C. Walkever (Ed.), *Assessment of learning assistance services. New directions for college learning assistance.* San Francisco: Jossey-Bass, 17-32.

Coda-Messerle, M. (1973). Data collection: A cybernetic aspect of a learning assistance center. In G. Kerstiens (Ed.), *Technological alternatives in learning.* Sixth annual proceedings of the Western College Reading Association, 6, 51-58.

Gerkin, D. M. (1995). *Student perceptions of the effectiveness of selected non-traditional programs at Paradise Valley Community College.* Master's Thesis, Ottawa University.

Gerkin, D. M. (1998). *Program evaluation in the learning assistance center at Paradise Valley Community College.* Unpublished paper presented at the 1999 Winter Institute for Learning Assistance Center Professionals, Tucson, AZ.

Maxwell, M. (1990). "Does tutoring help?" A look at the literature. *Review of Research in Developmental Education, 7,* (4), 1-5.

Maxwell, M. (1991). *Evaluating academic skills programs: A source book.* Kensington, MD, M.M. Associates.

Myers, C., & Majer, K. (1981). Using research designs to evaluate learning assistance programs. In C. Walkever (Ed.), *Assessment of learning assistance services. New directions for college learning assistance.* San Francisco: Jossey-Bass, 65-74.

Roueche, S. D. (1983). Elements of program success: Report of a national study. In J. E. Roueche (Ed.), *A new look at successful programs. New directions for college learning assistance.* San Francisco: Jossey-Bass, 3-10.

Spivey, N. (1981). Goal attainment scaling in the college learning center. *Journal of Developmental & Remedial Education,* (4), 2, 11-13.

Van, B. (1992). College learning assistance programs: Ingredients for success. *Journal of College Reading and Learning,* (24), 2, 27-39.

Vincent, V. C. (1983). *Impact of a college learning assistance center on the achievement and retention of disadvantaged students.* ED 283 438.

David M. Gerkin was born in Fitchburg, Massachusetts on November 15, 1956 and has resided in Phoenix, Arizona since 1963. He received his elementary education in Fitchburg and Phoenix and graduated from Moon Valley High School in 1974. He received an Associate of Arts degree in 1990 from Scottsdale Community College and an Associate of General Studies degree with high honors from Paradise Valley Community College in 1991. Mr. Gerkin began attending Ottawa University in the fall of 1992 and graduated with a Bachelor of Arts degree with a major in Adult Education in 1994. He received his Master of Arts in Counseling from Ottawa University in 1995. He received the Professional Staff Employee of the Year Award in 1993 from Paradise Valley Community College when he was employed as a Learning Technician in the Learning Assistance Center. Mr. Gerkin currently holds the position of Director of the Learning Support Center at Paradise Valley Community College. His professional areas of interest include tutor training, learning styles, study strategies, leadership development, and the transformation of post-secondary institutions into learning centered organizations. He is a guitar player, singer, and songwriter and enjoys spending time with his wife Aimée, his two teenage sons, Kyle and Noah, and his newborn son, Samuel.

Question #19:
How Do I Develop a Favorable Image for the LAC and How Do I Publicize the Programs and Services of the LAC?

A conversation with Frank L. Christ

Publicity is the art of developing materials and activities to announce and increase attendance at learning assistance programs and services. Publicity is aimed primarily at students and faculty.

Public relations attempts to create a favorable image of learning assistance staff, programs and services. Public relations, a broader activity than publicity, focuses on campus administrators, faculty, students, parents, and community.

Most efforts at publicity and public relations by many LAC administrators seem to be characterized by reluctance, false modesty, lack of objectives, absence of data, and evidence of its effectiveness.

Can we talk about publicity first? How do I get started publicizing my LAC?

Since you are starting a new center, I suggest that you focus on five major activities:
1. creating a description of the center and its programs and services for the campus catalog;
2. developing announcements in the campus newspaper and on campus radio, television, and web sites;
3. designing an LAC bookmark with essential program information that can be placed in textbooks of selected classes and also made available at selected campus locations;

4. briefing academic departments, related support programs like counseling, academic advising, orientation, and student associations and clubs that can lead to outcomes like faculty invitations to present to their classes, becoming a partner in orientation programs, and guest appearances at student meetings; and

5. placing signage both outside the center and on campus to direct people to the center.

A lot of what I am suggesting involves graphics and art. Use your campus art department and its students to help you with designing an LAC logo, your bookmarks, handouts, LAC interior walls and entrance graphics, and even T-shirts for LAC staff.

What about publicity for a center that I have been hired to direct?

First, I would find out what has already been done by looking through the campus catalog, reading back issues of the campus newspaper, combing the center's files for correspondence, art work, and copy relating to past publicity efforts. Then, use what is acceptable to you and your staff; revise material to reflect your views of the center's role; and write new copy to announce that you are the new LAC program administrator and describe your plans for its programs and services.

And before I forget, if the center had a mission statement with goals and objectives, review it. Revise and refine it to give you tasks and expected outcomes that will publicize the center. If there is no mission statement, write one and specify tasks, timelines, and staff responsible for each objective.

I think I have enough to get me started with the center's publicity. What about program image—what you call "public relations"?

Personally, I think public relations involves developing a campus network that includes every significant administrator, faculty member, and student leader as well as media and news people both on and off campus.

How do I go about developing a campus network?

Before answering, let's define your campus network as identified individuals on your campus who can help in some way to make your program successful. You can define your network by making a list to identify those campus individuals, scheduling and delegating networking activities, maintaining a networking activities log, reviewing the networking activities log periodically, and revising your list semesterly.

Can you describe how I would go about doing this?

Sure. Networking should be written as an annual goal with objectives, tasks, timelines, and staff members responsible.

Oh, and another thing. You might consider developing a secondary network of off-campus people and groups that can impact on your campus image. For example, meet with United Way and senior citizen groups for volunteers, other local colleges, local high schools, reporters from local newspapers, special interest groups like computer clubs, and college alumni officers.

Use that network to let everyone know how wonderful your center, its programs and services, and staff are.

Wait a minute. "Wonderful" is a fuzzy word. What do you mean by "wonderful"?

Well, "wonderful" has a different meaning for different people in your network. For your president—yes, he/she is part of your network—and for other senior administrators and faculty, "wonderful" means academic visibility and recognition through professional activities and awards. Every professional conference that you attend; every association office that you are elected to; every article, letter to the editor, book or software review, textbook or software program that you author or co-author; and every award and honor given you—and by the way, "you" includes every member of your staff—should be brought to their attention by correspondence and also submitted to campus and local media for publication.

Starting a Learning Assistance Center 95

What can I do to achieve academic credibility and enhance my program's image?

You can serve on university LAC committees, especially ones dealing with retention and orientation. You might also consider developing an LAC advisory board composed of faculty and student leaders. Both of these activities give you visibility at a high level on your campus.

You can network with high schools and community colleges in your area. You can impact on the local community by being part of a campus or community speaker's bureau and making presentations on learning assistance and by giving workshops on skills such as time management, speed reading, computer literacy.

A final few words. As director of the Learning Assistance Support System at CSU Long Beach, a program respected both on-campus and nationally, I made publicity and public relations happen by specifying annual objectives. To demonstrate our accountability in reaching these objectives, I started and maintained a series of large scrapbooks containing news copy relating to the LAC. These scrapbooks were evidence of completed publicity and public relations tasks by the LAC. They also came in handy when we wrote our annual reports.

ADDITIONAL READINGS

Christ, F. L. (1979). An audio tour of a university learning assistance center. *Technological Horizons in Education*, (6), 1, 50-51.

Knight, B., & Helm, P. (1981). Developing trustee commitment to learning assistance. In F. Christ & M. Coda-Messerle (Eds.). *Staff development for learning support systems. New directions for college learning assistance.* San Francisco: Jossey-Bass, 19-27.

Lowenstein, S. (1993). Using advisory boards for learning assistance programs. In *Perspectives on Practice in Developmental Education*. New York College Learning Skills Association.

Maxwell, M. (1997). Attracting students and developing a positive image. In *Improving student learning skills: A new edition.* Clearwater, FL: H&H Publishing Company.

Frank L. Christ has been with CRLA all of its existence beginning as a founding member in 1966 when he was at Loyola University, Los Angeles. Frank is a Past President (1968-69), editor of two WCRLA Proceedings (Combined Proceedings of the First, Second, and Third Annual Conferences and Proceedings of the Fourth Annual Conference, Newsletter Editorial Advisory Committee (1968-71), author of six articles, six of which were published in the association proceedings, recipient of Distinguished Leadership Award (1970), Distinguished Service Award (1972), and Long and Outstanding Service Award (1986). Frank coined the phrases; "Learning Assistance Support System," "Learning Assistance Center," and "Learning Assistance" in a 1971 CRLA article. Frank was the director of the Learning Assistance Support System at CSU–Long Beach from 1972-1989 and is presently a Visiting Scholar with the University Learning Center, University of Arizona, where he co-directs the annual Winter Institute for Learning Assistance Directors and Practitioners. His email address is flchris@primenet.com.

QUESTION #20:
ARE THERE STANDARDS FOR LEARNING ASSISTANCE PROGRAMS AND SERVICES?

A conversation with Georgine Materniak

Yes, there are some standards documents which are of interest to learning assistance professionals. The CAS (Council for the Advancement of Standards in Higher Education) *Standards for Learning Assistance Programs*, initially published in 1986 and revised in 1997, was the first document to set forth standards of practice for the profession. Other standards include the NADE (National Association of Developmental Education) *Self-Evaluation Guides* and the AMATYC (American Mathematical Association of Two-Year Colleges) *Standards for Introductory College Mathematics before Calculus*. Both the NADE *Guides* and AMATYC *Standards* were published in 1995.

What is the difference between the CAS Standards, NADE Guides, and AMATYC Standards?

The CAS *Standards* are used to assess an entire learning assistance program. The NADE *Guides* adopted the CAS format and applied it to self-assessment documents for four specific components found within learning centers. The NADE *Guides*, therefore, are component-specific standards and are used to assess tutoring services, adjunct instruction programs such as Supplemental Instruction, developmental courses, and the teaching/learning process. The AMATYC *Standards* are also component-specific and are used to establish standards of practice in college introductory mathematics courses.

So, you would use the CAS *Standards* to examine an entire program and the NADE *Guides* and AMATYC *Standards* to study particular components within the program.

What is the purpose of standards?

The primary purpose of standards is to promote quality programs and services for our students. Standards identify and articulate essential and necessary practices and elements found in good programs. The quality of a program can be determined by the degree to which these practices and elements are found in the program. Since we strive for excellence in meeting the needs of our students, we can use the standards to assure that our programs contain the essential ingredients found in high quality programs.

Why should I consider using standards?

Standards can be used for several purposes. Standards are used as tools for conducting a self-study of a program or a program component. Program self-studies are most often conducted in preparation for institutional accreditation. Standards are also used as a guide or checklist for developing a new program or for significantly expanding or consolidating existing services. For example, a tutor service that is charged with becoming a full-scale learning center would find the CAS *Standards* to be a good source for outlining the considerations and decisions that will need to be addressed. In addition to program development, standards can be used for staff development and provide a common focus for planning and goal setting exercises. Standards also function as an authoritative source for negotiating and bargaining with institutional administrators for additional resources or for justifying the continuation of certain program practices.

The NADE *Guides* suggest additional uses including serving as a discussion tool for program decisions, identifying a program component's strengths and weaknesses, formulating long-range planning, and making budget decisions.

What exactly is CAS?

CAS, which formed in 1979 as the Council for the Advancement of Standards for Student Services/Development Programs, was established as a consortium of student affairs professional organizations. In 1992, CAS broadened its scope and changed its name to Council for Advancement in Standards in Higher Education. NADE and CRLA then became members and actively involved in the planning and review of the document.

Can you describe the CAS Standards?

The CAS *Standards* are actually a collection of 23 documents that address specific functional areas in higher education. The learning assistance document is one of these 23 standards.

What is the format of the NADE Guides?

The NADE Standards and Evaluation Committee adopted the CAS Self-Assessment Guides format for creating the NADE *Self-Evaluation Guides* for Tutor Services, Adjunct Instructional Programs, Developmental Coursework Programs, and Program Factors Influencing the Teaching/Learning Process.

The Tutor Services Guide, for example, is made up of the same 13 sections found in the CAS Standards beginning with a "Mission" section and ending with the "Evaluation" section. However, the standards for each of these sections is written as an individual statement as found in the CAS Self-Assessment Guides format. Each section culminates in a summary which identifies areas of strengths and weaknesses and calls for specific action plans based on the assessment.

CAS Information:

How to get copies of the various standards documents:

To order the CAS *Standards* send $25 ($22 plus $3 postage and handling) in the form of a check or money order to:

CAS c/o ACPA
One Dupont Circle, NW, Ste. 300
Washington, DC 20036-1110

After September of 1998, the CAS *Standards* will be released for posting on web sites of major learning assistance organizations. Most likely, you will find it posted on the NADE, CRLA and Winter Institute web sites.

To order the NADE *Self-Evaluation Guides*, send $18.95 plus $5.00 shipping to:

H&H Publishing Company
1231 Kapp Drive
Clearwater, FL 33765
(727) 442-2195 for FAX with PO
(800) 366-4079 for phone with PO

Crossroads in Mathematics: Standards for Introductory College Mathematics Before Calculus can be ordered through:

AMATYC
State Technical Institute at Memphis
5983 Macon Cove
Memphis, TN 38134

Originally, *Crossroads in Mathematics* was made available free but the order form indicates that when the supply is exhausted, copies would be available at a moderate cost.

ADDITIONAL READINGS

Clark-Thayer, S. (Ed.). 1995. *NADE self-evaluation guides: Models for assessing learning assistance/ developmental education programs.* Clearwater, FL: H&H Publishing Company.

Cohen, D. (Ed.). 1995. *Crossroads in mathematics: Standards for introductory college mathematics before calculus.* Memphis, TN: American Mathematical Association for Two-Year Colleges.

Materniak G., & Williams, A. (1987). CAS standards and guidelines for learning assistance programs. *Journal of Developmental Education*, (11), 12-18.

Miller, T. K. (Ed.). 1997. *The book of professional standards for higher education.* Washington, DC: Council for the Advancement of Standards in Higher Education.

Georgine Materniak is the Director of the University of Pittsburgh Learning Skills Center. She has been active in professional organizations over the past 20 years first as Chairperson of ACPAUs Commission on Learning Centers in Higher Education and most recently as Co-Chair of the NADE Standards and Evaluation Committee. In these capacities, Georgine has been involved with program standards and certification projects. She was the primary drafter of the 1986 edition of the CAS Standards and Guidelines for Learning Assistance Centers and had significant responsibility for the 1997 revised edition. Georgine is a member of the team responsible for the NADE Program Certification project. She also serves on the editorial board of Learning Assistance Review.

Appendix A:
Typical Scenarios of a Learning Assistance Center Administrator

Scenarios by Karen G. Smith & Rick A. Sheets

Below are twenty common scenarios which new and experienced LAC administrators may face. Many of the scenarios are politically charged. Often new ideas are expected to be implemented using limited new money or with existing institutional resources. These are provided to provoke critical thinking and problem-solving. We welcome you to deal with one or more of the scenarios. Feel free to change any part of it to better fit a scenario you would like to address.

1. The vice president has set aside a small amount of money to support a program focused on improving retention for first and second year students. The focus for this retention program has been left entirely to you as you face a goal of demonstrating actual improved retention from first to second year. What are your first steps?

2. To prepare for the institution's renewal for accreditation, you and other administrators have been asked to develop a self-study for your areas. The self-study is to include statistics on purpose, use, and success. How would you proceed? What information would you include and how would you gather and report it?

3. A committee was appointed by the president of the faculty senate to study the feasibility for initiating a learning assistance center. After visits by committee members to existing programs and developing a plan based on LAC success stories from other universities, a consult-

ant was hired to draft a final plan, and you were hired or appointed to implement their plan. Please describe their plan and how you plan to implement it.

4. You have been invited to teach in a learning communities program with a biology instructor. The suggestion is that students will be required to sign up for both the study strategies and the biology course. You and the biology instructor will team-teach both courses to help give students a context to apply the study strategies being taught. How can the two be taught in an integrated fashion so that each of the two courses supports the other? How would you design the study skills course and how would it connect to the biology course?

5. You have just been hired to run an existing center. Most of the tutors are peer tutors and the only training has been a single staff meeting to present procedures for filling out time sheets for pay. You have been asked to develop and implement a comprehensive training program for your tutors. Describe the topics, delivery mode, funding, competencies, amount of training, short and long term planning, and any other aspects of how you would build a comprehensive training program?

6. In answer to a study of institutional responsiveness to students of minority and underrepresented populations, the college provost has decided that the greatest need for these students is the establishment of an LAC. You have been hired to respond to this special need while providing access to all students in the institution. What recommendations would you make (include services, staffing, funding, placement in organization, reporting structure, and evaluation process)?

7. A successful TRIO (federally-funded) program has been in operation for years at this college, providing support services to first-generation students from families with significant financial need, and the chief academic officer has decided to expand the program to serve all students by providing additional funding. As the director of the TRIO program you are faced with this new challenge. How would you plan to meet the federal guidelines as the project students are served while expanding and serving all students equally (include your proposal guidelines which may address any additional funding, staffing, service, or space considerations or requests)?

8. Your president has just returned from a national conference and is excited about the new concept of becoming a learner-centered institution. It is a new paradigm and has already become a hot issue because the focus becomes student learning rather than delivery of instruction. Your president has asked you to form a committee and lead the charge to develop a plan to follow and tout this new learner–centered model. Who would you ask to be on the committee? How would you "lead the charge"? What would you plan to accomplish (short and long term)?

9. In response to competition for new students, the chancellor is looking at distance education courses as a way to recruit and retain more students. Because of your reported success with retaining students using your center, she has asked you to develop strategies for recruiting and retaining students enrolled in distance education courses. What questions would you deal with? What assumptions are you making? Describe what suggestions you would make and why. What, if anything, have you chosen not to deal with and why?

10. Although the learning assistance center which you direct has been successful in providing appropriate services and programs, an institutional retrenchment has forced every unit and every department to reassess how services are funded and delivered. As the administrator for this LAC, you have been required to demonstrate how the unit can be reorganized so that services are not curtailed nor diminished while receiving less funding. Describe what you would do.

11. The president of the university, in his fund raising zeal, has convinced a friend/benefactor to give a major gift to the institution for the purpose of establishing a comprehensive learning assistance center. Because the center will carry the benefactor's name and could easily become a trophy-piece of the president, the development of programs and services is extremely sensitive and political. How would you balance institutional service needs with the potential political agenda? Describe what you see as a realistic plan and outcome. What else could be involved to make this a success and how do you define success?

12. Your institution is in the process of developing a comprehensive web site to encourage student interaction for institutional information, course

selection, registration, and some distance education options. You have been asked to develop a web page for your center. What will you identify as its purpose and function? What information or resources will your web page include? What opportunities for student interaction will be provided? How can it be used to better support your tutors and/or students?

13. While a long-time learning assistance center with little direction and/or inspiration has functioned insignificantly on campus, serving a limited number of students, the supervising vice-president sees the pending retirement of the current director as an opportunity to breathe new life into a potentially dynamic service. You have been hired to provide vision and develop meaningful services, but with very little additional funding. How would you approach this? Describe desired short and long term outcomes.

14. The number of students at your institution has decreased over the last two years and all departments have been asked to cut their budgets by ten percent. During the same period, the number of students using your services has actually increased by ten percent and the reported retention rate has also increased. How would you respond? Describe the reason for your response and the desired outcomes.

15. You are informed that some grant money has not been expended at your institution and that you have $25,000 to spend on new hardware and software to support your program. However, all money must be spent within the next six weeks. How would you decide what to purchase? Describe why you made the choices, who was involved in the decisions, and the "added value" of the purchases you made. What criteria would you suggest others look at in making similar decisions?

16. Your institution has very limited new money available to remodel some of the student and academic service areas on campus. It has been suggested that the remodeling include a merging of the library, media department, student-use computer lab, and the learning assistance center into one building. You have been asked to chair the campus representatives from each area and develop an effective model for integrating these services into the new building. Describe the issues your team will face, the process you would use to accomplish

this, and what you would see as a successful outcome of this committee. What suggestions would you have for others in a similar situation?

17. A powerful faculty member on your campus is critical of the new learning assistance center program you have presented. He has raised some concerns with fellow faculty which include concerns about:
    ◊ additional funding needed for this program;
    ◊ students' responsibility versus the institution's;
    ◊ amateurs providing instruction; and
    ◊ loss of face of faculty involved in the LAC program.
    How would you answer these concerns? Why? If this were an ideal situation, what would be different?

18. You suggested your institution create a tutoring program. With little additional funding and the addition of a work-study student for the program, you have been asked to develop a three-year plan for implementing this new program. Describe your plan and include staffing, equipment, and funding considerations. Describe why you made the choices you did.

19. A faculty member has come to you with a proposal to develop an on-line tutoring option for students in her distance education courses. She will create the web pages and lead the charge for other interested faculty. What is your role in supporting her efforts and helping her establish this new option for students? What equipment, staffing, and other considerations need to be included in this planning stage?

20. Several faculty members have complained that there is no make-up testing facility and have asked if your center could provide that as a service to students. No one has identified additional funding. However, some additional space may be available. What would you propose? What would be an ideal situation and how would it differ from what you described?

The previous scenarios were intended to present a variety of real-life situations. Though some of the specifics may change, the general tone or themes of the scenarios are prevalent in centers today. The key to dealing with any of the scenarios is in the planning, the network of support to implement, and the documentation and evaluation of the level of success with "next step" recommendations.

APPENDIX B:
BIBLIOGRAPHY AND ADDITIONAL READINGS

Baker, G., & Painter, P. L. (1983). The learning center: A study of effectiveness. In J. E. Roueche (Ed.), *A new look at successful programs. New directions for college learning assistance.* San Francisco: Jossey- Bass, 73-88.

Beal, P. E. (1980). Learning centers and retention. In O. T. Lenning & D. L. Wayman (Eds.). *New roles for learning assistance. New directions for college learning assistance.* San Francisco: Jossey-Bass, 59-73.

Biggs, J. B. (1993). What do inventories of students' learning processes really measure? A theoretical review and a clarification. *British Journal of Educational Psychology,* (63), 3-19.

Blanchard, K., & Bowles, S. (1997). *Gung ho!: Turn on the people in any organization.* New York: William Morrow & Company.

Bliss, L., & Mueller, R. (1994). *SBI (Study Behaviors Inventory).* Rancho Palos Verdes, CA: Andragogy Associates.

Briggs, K., & Briggs Myers, I. (1990). *MBTI (Myers-Briggs Type Indicator).* Palo Alto, CA: Consulting Psychologists Press, Inc.

Brown, R. R. (1980). Evaluating learning centers. In O.T. Lenning & R. Nayman (Eds.). *New roles for learning assistance. New directions for college learning assistance.* San Francisco: Jossey-Bass, 75-92.

Brown, W. C. (1982). College learning assistance: A developmental concept. *Journal of College Student Personnel* (September), 395-401.

Brown, S., Carnahan, W., Kerstiens, G., & Maddaford, H. (1977). Technology with humanism supports learning. *Community and Junior College Journal,* 6-8, 27.

Burns, J. M. (1978). *Leadership.* New York: Harper and Row Publishers.

Burns, M. E. (1986). Management strategies to assist students in improving learning skills. *Journal of Developmental Education,* (9), 3, 2-4.

Burns, M. E. (1987). *Leadership styles and management skills of learning assistance/developmental education program directors/coordinators.* ERIC ED288472.

Burns, M. E. (1993). A study to formulate a learning assistance model for the California community college. In S. Mioduski & G. Enright (Eds.). *Proceedings of the 13th and 14th annual institutes for learning assistance professionals.* Tucson: University Learning Center, University of Arizona, 20-23.

Burns-Reed, M. E., & Dozen, P. (1982). New partnerships in academe. In H. Boylan (Ed.), *Forging new partnerships in learning assistance. New directions for college learning assistance.* San Francisco: Jossey-Bass, 17-29.

Caputo, E. (1989). Learning center model and administration. *Issues in College Learning Centers, (9)*, 55-61.

Carlson, R., & Bailey, J. (1997). *Slowing down to the speed of life.* New York: Harper Collins.

Carpenter, K. (1985). A place for learning centers in the administrative structure of postsecondary institutions. *Forum for Reading, 17,* 1, 23-27.

Casazza, M. E., & Silverman, S. L. (1996). *Learning assistance and developmental education: A guide for effective practice.* San Francisco: Jossey-Bass.

Castelli, C., & De Johnson. (1984). Learning center assessment: Managing for change in the 80's. In D. R. Fleming (Ed.), *Journal of College Reading and Learning, 17,* 30-42.

Caverly, D. (1995). Technology and the learning assistance center. In S. Mioduski & G. Enright (Eds.). *Proceedings of the 15th and 16th annual institutes for learning assistance professionals,* 1-14.

Caverly, D. (1995). Technology in learning centers: Past, present, future. In S. Mioduski & G. Enright (Eds.). *Proceedings of the 15th and 16th annual institutes for learning assistance professionals,* 15-34.

Caverly, D. (1997). Teaching reading in a learning assistance center. In S. Mioduski & G. Enright (Eds.). *Proceedings of the 17th and 18th annual institutes for learning assistance professionals,* 27-42.

Caverly, D., & Flippo, R. (1991). *Teaching reading and study strategies at the college level.* International Reading Association.

Chickering, A. (1990). *Education and identity.* San Francisco: Jossey-Bass.

Chickering, A., and others. (1990). *The modern American college.* San Francisco: Jossey-Bass.

Christ, A. A. (1977). Videotaping: A useful technique for learning assistance practitioners. In G. Enright (Ed.), *Personalizing learning systems: Ecologies and strategies.* Proceedings of the tenth annual conference of the Western College Reading Association, 10, 115-118.

Christ, F. L. (1971). Systems for learning assistance: Learners, learning facilitators, and learning centers. In F. L. Christ (Ed.), *Interdisciplinary aspects of reading instruction.* Fourth annual proceedings of the Western College Reading Association, 32-41.

Christ, F. L. (1972). Preparing practitioners, counselors, and directors of college learning assistance centers. In F. P. Greene (Ed.), *College reading: Problems and programs of junior and senior colleges.* Twenty-first yearbook of the National Reading Conference, 2, 179-188.

Christ, F. L. (1977). Management of a learning assistance sector. In G. Enright (Ed.), *Personalizing learning systems: Ecologies and strategies.* Tenth annual proceedings of the Western College Reading Association, 76-84.

Christ, F. L. (1978). Management is evaluation. *Audiovisual Instruction, (23),* 8, 26, 62.

Christ, F. L. (1979). An audio tour of a university learning assistance center. *Technological Horizons in Education,* 6, 1, 50-51.

Christ, F. L. (1980) Learning assistance at a state university: A cybernetic model. In K. V. Lauridsen (Ed.), *Examining the scope of learning centers. New directions for college learning assistance*, 45-56.

Christ, F. L. (1982). Computers in learning assistance centers and developmental education: Beginning to explore. *Journal of Developmental & Remedial Education*, 10-13.

Christ, F. L. (1985). *SRSE II (Survey of Reading/Study Efficiency)*. Sierra Vista, AZ: Personal Efficiency Programs.

Christ, F. L. (1994). Yesterday's words, tomorrow's challenges. In S. Mioduski & G. Enright (Eds.), *Proceedings of the 13th and 14th annual institutes for learning assistance professionals: 1992 and 1993*. Tucson, AZ: University Learning Center, University of Arizona, 9-11.

Christ, F. L. (1997). Using MBO to create, develop, improve, and sustain learning assistance programs. In S. Mioduski & G. Enright (Eds.). *Proceedings of the 17th and 18th annual institutes for learning assistance professionals*, 43-51.

Clark, E. A. (1980). The learning center in the urban university. In K. V. Lauridsen (Ed.), *Examining the scope of learning centers. New directions for college learning assistance*. San Francisco: Jossey-Bass, 9-17.

Clark-Thayer, S. (Ed.). 1995. *NADE self-evaluation guides: Models for assessing learning assistance/developmental education programs*. Clearwater, FL: H&H Publishing Company.

Clowes, D. (1981). Evaluation methodologies for learning assistance programs. In C. Walkever (Ed.), *Assessment of learning assistance services. New directions for college learning assistance*. San Francisco: Jossey-Bass, 17-32.

Coda-Messerle, M. (1973). Data collection: A cybernetic aspect of a learning assistance center. In G. Kerstiens (Ed.), *Technological alternatives in learning*. Sixth annual proceedings of the Western College Reading Association, 6, 51-58.

Coda-Messerle, M. D. (1980). Professional resources for learning assistance specialists. In K. V. Lauridsen (Ed.), *Examining the scope of learning centers. New directions for college learning assistance*. San Francisco: Jossey-Bass, 87-98.

Cohen, D. (Ed.). 1995. *Crossroads in mathematics: Standards for introductory college mathematics before calculus*. Memphis, TN: American Mathematical Association for Two-Year Colleges.

Commander, N. E., Stratton, C. B., Callahan, C. A., & Smith, B. D. (1996). A learning assistance model for expanding academic support, *Journal of Developmental Education, 20*, (2), 8-10, 12, 14, 16.

Covey, S. (1990). *7 habits of highly effective people: Powerful lessons in personal change*. New York: Simon & Schuster.

Covey, S. R. (1992). *Principled centered leadership*. New York: Summit Books.

Covey, S. R. (1994). *First things first*. New York: Simon and Shuster, 103-117.

Dempsey, J., & Tomlinson, B. (1980). Learning centers and instructional/curricular reform. In O. T. Lenning & R. T. Nayman (Eds.). *New roles for learning assistance*. San Francisco: Jossey-Bass, 41-58.

Enright, G. (1995). LAC, LRC, and developmental education: An orientation for the beginning learning center professional. In S. Mioduski and G. Enright (Eds.). *Proceedings of the 15th and 16th annual institutes for learning assistance professionals*, 40-47.

Enright, G., & Kerstiens, G. (1980). The learning center: Toward an expanded role. In O. T. Lenning & R I. Nayman (Eds.). *New roles for learning assistance. New directions for college learning assistance*, San Francisco: Jossey-Bass, 1-24.

Flippo, R. F., & Caverly, D. C. (2000). *Handbook of college reading and study strategy research*. Mahway, NJ: Lawrence Erlbaum Publishers.

Fujitaki, N. (1974). CSULB intern training in learning assistance. In G. Kerstiens (Ed.), *Reading update: Ideals to reality*. Seventh annual proceedings of the Western College Reading Association, 83-90.

Gabriel, D. (1989). Assessing assessment. *Review of Research in Developmental Education*, 6 (5), 1-6.

Garcia, S. (1981). The training of learning assistance practitioners. In F. L. Christ & M. Coda-Messerle (Eds.). *Staff development for learning support systems. New directions for college learning assistance*. San Francisco: Jossey-Bass, 4, 29-37.

Garner, A. (1980). A comprehensive community college model for learning assistance centers. In K.V. Lauridsen (Ed.), *Examining the scope of learning centers. New directions for college learning assistance*. San Francisco: Jossey-Bass, 19-31.

Gerkin, D. M. (1995). *Student perceptions of the effectiveness of selected non-traditional programs at Paradise Valley Community College*. Master's Thesis, Ottawa University.

Gerkin, D. M. (1998). *Program evaluation in the learning assistance center at Paradise Valley Community College*. Unpublished paper presented at the 1999 Winter Institute for Learning Assistance Center Professionals, Tucson, AZ.

Godsey, E. (1992). *The functions of a learning center*. Unpublished doctoral dissertation, Southern Missouri University.

Hashway, R. M. (1989). Developmental learning center designs. *Research and Teaching in Developmental Education*, (5), 2, 25-38.

Heard, P. (1976). College learning specialists: A profession coming of age. In *Proceedings of the ninth annual conference of the Western College Reading Association*, 1-9.

Jones, L. B. (1996). *The path: Creating your mission statement for work and for life*. New York: Hyperion.

Karwin, T. J. (1973). *Flying a learning center: Design and costs of an off-campus space for learning*. Berkeley, CA: Carnegie Commission on Higher Education.

Kemig, R.T. (1983). Raising academic standards: A guide to learning improvement. *AAHE/ERIC Education Research Report No. 4.* Washington, D.C.: American Association for Higher Education.

Kerstiens, G. (1972). The ombudsman function of the college learning center. In F. Greene (Ed.), *College reading: Problems and programs of junior and senior colleges.* Twenty-first yearbook of the National Reading Conference, 2, 221-227.

Kerstiens, G. (1994). Postsecondary student assessment and placement: History, status, direction. In S. Mioduski & G. Enright (Eds.). *Proceedings of the 13th and 14th annual institutes for learning assistance professionals*, 56-62.

Kerstiens, G. (1995). A taxonomy of learning support services. In S. Mioduski & G. Enright (Eds.). *Proceedings of the 15th and 16th annual institutes for learning assistance professionals,* 48-51.

Knight, B., & Helm, P. (1981). Developing trustee commitment to learning assistance. In F. Christ & M. Coda-Messerle (Eds.). *Staff development for learning support systems. New directions for college learning assistance.* San Francisco: Jossey Bass, 19-27.

Knowles, M. (1984). *Andragogy in action.* San Francisco: Jossey-Bass.

Knowles, M. (1988). *The modern practice of adult education.* Cambridge, MA: Cambridge University Press.

Knowles, M. (1998). *The adult learner (4th Ed).* Gulf Publications.

Lissner, L. S. (1989). College learning assistance programs: The results of a national survey. *Issues in College Learning Centers*, 9, 82-95.

Lissner, L. S. (1990). The learning center from 1829 to the year 2000 and beyond. In R. M. Hashway (Ed.), *Handbook of developmental education.* New York: Praeger Publishers, 127-154.

Lowenstein, S. (1993). Using advisory boards for learning assistance programs. In *Perspectives on Practice in Developmental Education.* New York College Learning Skills Association.

Martin, D. C., Lorton, M., Blanc, R., & Evans, C. (1978). *The learning center: A comprehensive model for colleges and universities.* Kansas City, MO: Student Learning Center, University of Missouri, ERIC ED 162-294.

Martin, D. C. (1980). Learning centers in professional schools. In K. V. Lauridsen (Ed.), *Examining the scope of learning centers. New directions for college learning assistance.* San Francisco: Jossey-Bass, 69-79.

Martin, D. C., & Blanc, R. (1980). The learning center's role in retention: Integrating student support services with departmental instruction. *Journal of Developmental & Remedial Education,* (4), 2-4.

Materniak G., & Williams, A. (1987). CAS standards and guidelines for learning assistance programs. *Journal of Developmental Education,* (11), 12-18.

Matthews, J. M. (1981). Becoming professional in college level learning assistance. In F. Christ & M. Coda-Messerle (Eds.). *Staff development for learning support systems. New directions for college learning assistance.* San Francisco: Jossey Bass, 1-18.

Maxwell, M. (1978). *Improving student learning skills*. San Francisco: Jossey-Bass.

Maxwell, M. (1981). An annual institute for directors and staff of college learning centers. In F. Christ & M. Coda-Messerle (Eds.). *Staff development for learning support systems. New directions for college learning assistance*. San Francisco: Jossey Bass, 39-45.

Maxwell, M. (1990). "Does tutoring help?" A look at the literature. *Review of Research in Developmental Education, 7*, (4), 1-5.

Maxwell, M. (1991). *Evaluating academic skills programs: A source book*. Kensington, MD, M.M. Associates.

Maxwell, M. (1997). Attracting students and developing a positive image. In *Improving student learning skills: A new edition*. Clearwater, FL: H&H Publishing Company.

Maxwell, M. (1997). *Improving student learning skills: A new edition*. Clearwater, FL: H&H Publishing Company.

Maxwell, M. (1998). Fellows in learning assistance and developmental education: A proposal. *Journal of College Reading and Learning, 29*, (1), 41-47.

Milesko-Pytelin (1994). Total quality management in college learning centers. *Research & Teaching in Developmental Education, 11*, (1), 115-123.

Miller, C., Dean, J. F., & McKinley, D. L. 1990). Learning approaches and motives: Male and female differences and implications for learning assistance programs. *The Journal of College Student Development, 31*, 147-154.

Miller, T. K. (Ed.). 1997. *The book of professional standards for higher education*. Washington, DC: Council for the Advancement of Standards in Higher Education.

Myers, C., & Majer, K. (1981). Using research designs to evaluate learning assistance programs. In C. Walkever (Ed.), *Assessment of learning assistance services. New directions for college learning assistance*. San Francisco: Jossey-Bass, 65-74.

Odom, M. L. (1992). *Incorporating new technologies into an academic assistance center*. Paper presented at fifth annual Midwest Regional Reading and Study Skills Conference, Kansas City, MO.

Paul, R. (1992). *Critical thinking*. Santa Rosa, CA: Foundation for Critical Thinking.

Peters, T. (1997). *The pursuit of WOW*. New York: Vintage Books.

Peterson, G. T. (1975). *The learning center: A sphere for nontraditional approaches to education*. Hamden, CT: Shoestring Press.

Pflug, R. J. (1973). The handicapped and disadvantaged students in the learning center. In G. Kerstiens (Ed.), *Technological alternatives in learning*. Proceedings of the sixth annual conference of the Western College Reading Association, 131-135.

Pintrich, P., Smith, D., Garcia, T., & McKeachie, W. (1991). *MSLQ (Motivated Strategies for Learning Questionnaire)*. Ann Arbor, MI: University of Michigan.

Roueche, S. D. (1983). Elements of program success: Report of a national study. In J. E. Roueche (Ed.), *A new look at successful programs. New directions for college learning assistance.* San Francisco: Jossey-Bass, 3-10.

Shaw, G. (1994). Multiple dimensions of academic support: One learning center's response to learning diversity. In R. Lemelin (Ed.), *Issues in access to higher education.* Portland, ME: University of Southern Maine, 14-16.

Shaw, J. (1980). Learning centers and the faculty: Improving academic competency. In O.T. Lenning & R. Nayman (Eds.). *New roles for learning assistance. New directions for college learning assistance,* (2), 25-39.

Sheets, R. A. (1994). *The effects of training and experience on adult peer tutors in community colleges.* Doctoral dissertation, Arizona State University, 1-5.

Sheets, R. A. (1997). 5 C's of learning assistance center director as manager: Compassion, commitment, connections, credibility, catalyst. In S. Mioduski & G. Enright (Eds.). *Proceedings of the 17th and 18th annual institutes for learning assistance professionals,* 82-84.

Sherr, L. A., & Teeter, D. J. (1991). *Total quality management in higher education.* San Francisco: Jossey-Bass.

Smith, G. D., Enright, G., & Devirian, M. (1975). A national survey of learning and study skills programs. In G. H. McNich & W. D. Miller (Eds.). *Reading: Convention and inquiry.* Clemson, SC: National Reading Conference Proceedings, 67-73.

Smith, K. (1995). Twelve key questions to answer and one critical issue in designing and implementing a collegiate learning center. In S. Mioduski & G. Enright (Eds.). *Proceedings of the 15th and 16th annual institutes for learning assistance professionals,* 54-55.

Smith, K., & Brown, S. (1981). Staff performance evaluation in learning assistance centers. In C. Walkever (Ed.), *Assessment of learning assistance services. New directions for college learning assistance.* San Francisco: Jossey-Bass, 95-110.

Smith, K. G., Clymer, C., & Brabham, R. D. (1976). Revolutionizing the attitudes of academia through a learning skills center. In R. Sugimoto (Ed.), *Revolutionizing college learning skills.* Proceedings of the ninth annual conference of the Western College Reading Association, 174-180.

Spivey, N. (1981). Goal attainment scaling in the college learning center. *Journal of Developmental & Remedial Education, (4),* 2, 11-13.

Van, B. (1992). College learning assistance programs: Ingredients for success. *Journal of College Reading and Learning, (24),* 2, 27-39.

Vincent,V. C. (1983). *Impact of a college learning assistance center on the achievement and retention of disadvantaged students.* ED 283 438.

Walker, C. (1980). The learning assistance center in a selective institution. In K. V. Lauridsen (Ed.), *Examining the scope of learning centers.* San Francisco: Jossey-Bass, 57-68.

Weinstein, C., Schulte, A., & Palmer, D. (1987). *LASSI (Learning & Study Strategies Inventory).* Clearwater, FL: H&H Publishing Company.

Weisberger, R. (1994). Model for the development of an academic support center. In I. Anderson (Ed.), *A sourcebook for developmental educators*. Manchester, NH: Learning Assistance Association of New England, 16-21.

Williams, G. H., Arnold, J. W., & Jacobsen, P. A. (1971). Prescriptive teaching linked to a learning and tutorial center. In F. L. Christ (Ed.), *Interdisciplinary aspects of reading instruction*. Fourth annual proceedings of the Western College Reading Association, 147-155.

White, W. G., Jr., & Schnuth, M. L. (1990). College learning assistance centers: Places for learning. In R. M. Hashway (Ed.), *Handbook of developmental education*. New York: Praeger, 155-177.

White, W. G., Jr., Kyzar, B., & Lane, K. E. (1990). College learning assistance centers: Spaces for learning. In R. M. Hashway (Ed.), *Handbook of developmental education*. New York: Praeger, 179-195.

White, W. G., Jr., Kyzar, B., & Lane, K. E. (1990). College learning assistance center design considerations. *The Educational Facility Planner, (28)*, 4, 22-26.

Whyte, C. S. (1980). An integrated counseling and learning center. In K.V.Lauridsen (Ed.), *Examining the scope of learning centers. New directions for college learning assistance*. San Francisco: Jossey-Bass, 33-43.

Xenakis, F. S. (1979). Learning assistance support system for disadvantaged nursing students. In G. Enright (Ed.), *Multicultural diversity and learning*. Twelfth Annual Proceedings of the Western College Reading Association, Vol. XII, Los Angeles, 128-132.

NOTE: For almost everything that relates to learning assistance centers, go to the Learning Support Center/Winter Institute Site at http://www.pvc.maricopa.edu/winterinstitute/ This web site includes a calendar of learning assistance related conferences, a directory of learning assistance related associations and listservs, many full text articles, and software and book reviews.

Starting a Learning Assistance Center

Conversations with CRLA members who have been there and done that!

ISBN 0-943202-72-8   ($21.95 + $5.00 Shipping)

H&H Publishing Order Form
Order by mail, phone, or fax with check, purchase order or VISA/MasterCard

Name: _____   Purchase Order #: _____

Credit Card #: _____   Exp. Date: _____

Institution: _____

Address: _____

City: _____   State: _____   Zip Code: _____

Phone: ( ) _____   E-mail: _____

H&H Publishing Company, Inc. **Phone: (800) 366-4079**
1231 Kapp Drive **Fax: (727) 442-2195**
Clearwater, FL 33765 **Web: www.HHPublishing.com**